REREADING LITERATURE
Alexander Pope

Alexander Pope

Laura Brown

Basil Blackwell

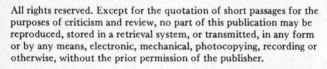

© Laura Brown 1985

First published 1985

Basil Blackwell Publisher Ltd
108 Cowley Road, Oxford OX4 1JF, UK

Basil Blackwell Inc.
432 Park Avenue South, Suite 1505,
New York, NY 10016, USA

British Library Cataloguing in Publication Data

Brown, Laura
    Alexander Pope.
    1. Pope, Alexander – Criticism and interpretation
    I. Title
    821'.5 PR 3634

    ISBN 0–631–13502–2
    ISBN 0–631–13503–0 Pbk

Library of Congress Cataloging in Publication Data

Brown, Laura, 1949–
    Alexander Pope.

    (Rereading literature)
    Includes index.
    1. Pope, Alexander, 1688–1744 – Criticism and interpretation.
    I. Title. II. Series.
    PR3634.B76 1985 821'.5 84–20317

    ISBN 0–631–13502–2
    ISBN 0–631–13503–0 Pbk

Typeset by Cambrian Typesetters, Frimley, Surrey
Printed in Great Britain by Whitstable Litho Ltd, Kent.

Contents

Editor's Preface

Few periods have proved as alluring to traditional English studies as the early eighteenth century. Since 'English' itself was established in the nineteenth century as a 'civilizing' discipline, a bulwark of spiritual harmony and eternal truth in an epoch of deep social conflict, what more natural than that it should model itself from the outset on the age of Pope, with its good sense and fine taste, its appeal to universal Reason, its passion for symmetry and stability? The ideological reading of the early eighteenth century we know as 'Augustanism', where the world was still a fit place for gentlemen, needed of course to edit out the less palatable social realities of the time: the squalour and exploitation, the material destitution and imperialist violence, even, from time to time, the embarrassingly vituperative excesses of its most admired authors, which hardly seemed wholly compatible with literary decorum. But it was not just a question of English studies constructing a past after its own image, though this was undoubtedly the case; it was also a matter of its obediently reproducing the *self-image* of a minority social group in early eighteenth-century England, one equally blinded to the determining social forces of which it was the privileged product. Once installed in place, 'Augustanism' provided at once a working model of what 'English' was meant to be about', and a consolatory golden age into which, besieged by the indecorous twentieth century, literary scholars could always beat a retreat. At the very centre of that charmed enclave were the silver-tongued couplets of Alexander Pope, which — gracefully purged of the odd splenetic paroxysm — could stand as nothing less than the embodiment of Nature and Reason.

The Pope constructed by Laura Brown's study is a radically different affair. It is a Pope whose poetry is less magically free of social and ideological contradiction than in part constituted by it; a Pope whose writing, in the very act of lending its voice to imperialist power and social oppression, finds itself curiously, unwittingly diverted into affirming something very like the opposite. Brown locates such conflicts in the very forms of Pope's work — in the ambivalence of a mode of imagery, or the dual connotations of a genre — and shows the place of such conflict in the ruling ideologies of the age. The Pope she yields us is one fascinating less for his authoritative assurance than for the richness of his uncertainties. After this powerful exercise in demystification, it should be less easy to mistake the patrician values of Alexander Pope — values already to some degree archaic in his own day — for the unchanging truths of the human heart.

Terry Eagleton

Preface

> ... fit for my own country, and
> for my own time.
> (Pope to Swift, 14 September 1725)

If this study is in any way a work 'fit for my own country, and for my own time', my students and colleagues at Cornell have made it so. I must first thank the Literature Club and in particular Bethany Schroeder for sponsoring the talk on *Windsor-Forest* that formed the germ of this reading of Pope. From that first essay to the various versions of the longer text, the book has profited from the comments and criticisms — some harsh, some circumspect and some admirably patient — of Cynthia Baughman, Fredric Bogel, Debra Fried, Neil Hertz, Suvir Kaul, Veronica Kelly, Donna Landry, Gerald Maclean, Shirley Samuels, Mark Seltzer and Harry Shaw. I am grateful to all these readers, and to those other friends who were willing to talk with me at length about the project. I must also thank my editor Philip Carpenter, as well as Claire Andrews of Blackwell's, for their assistance in the final stages of revision, and especially Terry Eagleton for the incentive to put my ideas on Pope into finished form and the opportunity to venture a strongly revisionist reading.

My largest debt is to Walter Cohen, to whom this book is dedicated.

Introduction

This book may seem at first like an attack on Alexander Pope. Perhaps it is. My difficult task, at last, will be to convert that attack into the most effective of appreciations. Whether I successfully appropriate my own indictment of Pope's poetry is best left to another judge, but the attempt at appropriation — the act of making something our own, of turning it to our own use despite its difference and distance from us — is common among readers of Pope and even among Pope's works themselves. My study is thus, at least in this sense, paradigmatic: the most typical book on Pope yet produced. But my act of appropriation, depending as it does upon indictment rather than advocacy, has a very different end from that of most readings of Pope's poetry.

Historically, criticism of Pope has moved from disparagement to appreciation. Only twelve years after Pope's death, Joseph Warton damned his work with the faint praise that 'in that species of poetry wherein POPE excelled, he is superior to all mankind: and I only say, that this species of poetry is not the most excellent one of the art.'[1] By 1782, in a later essay of Warton's, Pope had been decisively labelled with the second-class epithet: the 'Poet of Reason'.[2] Nineteenth-century readers, with only a few notable exceptions, joined in this dismissal of Pope's poetry. In Matthew Arnold's well-known formulation, 'though they may write in verse, though they may in a certain sense be masters of the art of versification, Dryden and Pope are not classics of our poetry, they are classics of our prose.'[3] Macaulay, among others, extended this attack on the poetry to Pope's defective nature, his 'bad heart', his characteristic 'frauds of malignity, of fear, of interest, and of vanity'.[4] |The recent flood of books on Pope, then, is the ultimate product of a retrieval effort that began in the first half of the twentieth century on two related fronts: the New Critical attempt to document the ambiguities, the complexities, the ironies and the richness of the poetry itself,[5] and the historicist effort to forestall modern distaste by urging the reader to become, at least for the nonce, Pope's 'ideal contemporary'[6] in cultural attitudes, in classical scholarship and in political and social beliefs. Though the New Critical approach is often pro-grammatically ahistorical, these two apparently opposite positions often appear together in Restoration and eighteenth-century studies, perhaps because the texts — especially those of Dryden and Pope — are so inaccessible that a New Critical reading cannot find its way to the rich-ness of the verse without an historical opening. In any case, criticism of Pope, even today, is still written under the threat of attack and dismissal. Readers of Pope's work must prove that the poetry is imagistically rich,[7] that it is intellectually coherent,[8] that it represents a complex subjectivity,[9] that it is humane,[10] visionary[11] and passionate.[12] Constructive attack is difficult in this climate. The only recent book to question Pope's current status fails to move beyond cavil and *ad hominem* complaint.[13] And, symptomatically, this attempt was itself attacked for applying extra-aesthetic standards to Pope's work, for judging Pope's morality rather than either placing the poems in a universal and therefore non-moral aesthetic category or learning to transcend historically produced differences in taste.[14]

Where do we stand if we do not take one of these two routes to appropriation: the aesthetic or the 'ideal con-temporary'? If we do not believe in Pope — either as a humanist, a moralist, a philosopher, a poetic genius, a cultural theorist or a political propagandist — how can we even begin to read his poems, much less make them our own? This book contends that we must begin on the offensive. As a consistent advocate of the beliefs and ambitions of the capitalist landlords and of an imperialist consensus, Pope must be scrutinized, doubted and demystified. That is, the explicit values — the conscious political, social and even aesthetic positions of his poetry — must be critically and remorselessly questioned. This process of demystification, with its systematic refusal to see things as Pope would have us see them, to accept the world as Pope constructs it or to accede to Pope's assertions of meaning, coherence and morality, can be described as a critique of ideology: a critique of the conscious or unconscious values of the poet and his poems. Such a critique is not an attack on Pope from the outside, from the wiser perspective of a later historical moment. It seeks instead to find in Pope's poems themselves the signs of their ideology, to define the structures of belief by which their systems of value are sustained. Examined in this way, with a respectful lack of sympathy, Pope's poems tell us more about the age — its art, its ethics, and its 'humanity' — than Pope ever intended. Indeed, Pope's major works stand as documents of the ideological structures of the period, and if we read them not for what they claim to say but for what they fail to recognize, what they rationalize away, what they carefully conceal, and for the complex process by which they conceal it, we can begin to identify a new basis on which to understand their significance.

My attack on Pope, then, is designed to recover a set of historical insights from Pope's poetry. Specifically, it is designed to open up the two key issues of early eighteenth-century history and of Pope's work: the interconnected developments of capitalism and mercantile imperialism. In its classic form as it appears after the industrial revolution, capitalism is perhaps best understood strictly as a process of production. In eighteenth-century England, however, this system is not yet fully in force, though many of the initial necessary preconditions and some of the actual productive relations are certainly present. For our purposes, then, the crucial historical consideration is not so much a fully developed capitalist production as the cultural impact of a system of generalized commodity exchange. I will therefore use 'capitalist' loosely to include such matters as money, trade, economic self-interest and, perhaps most important, commodification — the transformation of things, people, social relations and, in Pope's case, even animals and actions as well as literary texts themselves into objects of exchange. Imperialism, especially as it arose in seventeenth- and eighteenth-century England, can be seen as the international dimension or extension of early capitalism, in which the exploitation of less developed societies, through trade and investment and backed by military force, becomes the source of profits and of commodities from around the world.

History, then, is the central reference point for this particular appropriation of Pope. But, as we shall see, history is not simply an objective externality that Pope's works faithfully imitate, nor is it a determining extrinsic force that dictates the shape of the poems. History is Pope's poetry, in the sense that these poems construct a version of history for their age. The history they produce bears an ultimate relation to the dominant social and economic event of the time — to the dual development of capitalism and imperialism. But it is also their own story, distinctively shaped and rendered, endowed with a unique imagery and language and a peculiar logic, through which the realities of eighteenth-century England are reordered, recoloured and even remade. We will thus be concerned first and last with the poems themselves. They will be our history, in the sense that I will take my lead in my reference to the historical and literary context of Pope's works from their own engagement with the realities of their world. Furthermore, this study is concerned not only with the explicit thematic statements or silences of the poetry, but also with its particular formal properties, the stylistic contours of the works. What *Windsor-Forest* says or fails to say about English imperialism and the politics of the Peace of Utrecht is no more important, for this analysis, than the underlying patterns of expression and description in which its statements are embodied. My reading, then, moves back and forth between stated beliefs and linguistic structures, between the political and social materials of Pope's major poetry and its typical forms. At some points Pope's language — and the parallel rhetorical devices of contemporary works — provides the main focus; at others the argument is primarily carried by the social and political beliefs and disbeliefs of the poetry. But taken as a whole, as a single — though certainly not a complete or exclusive — perspective on Pope, this study seeks to construct a continuously reciprocal reading of language and idea, a critique of ideology in which literary form is a constitutive category.

The discussion of the ideology of form in Pope's poetry opens up a variety of broader questions about the ideology of eighteenth-century literary form in general. Pope's works provide a distinctive political vantage point from which to view some of the period's most typical rhetorical structures — especially enumerative language and cataloguing — as well as some of the major neo-classical modes of the age — mock-heroic, georgic and *concordia discors*. And even local images — other worlds, new worlds, the Indian, the ocean, the fountain, the forest, the dancing trees, the whale and the dolphin, the harbour and the mole — recur throughout the literature of the period and gain a new ideological dimension from a discussion of their role in Pope's works. Pope has been the centre of the canon in traditional eighteenth-century literary history for good reason, it seems. This study keeps him there. But it keeps him as a subversive, as a lever against the whole canon of eighteenth-century studies. In that sense my reading is not a last word or a full or final evaluation, but barely a beginning, an essay towards that subversion.

1 Imperialism and Poetic Form:
The Rape of the Lock (1712, 1714, 1717),
Windsor-Forest (1713)

The most familiar couplet in all of Pope's corpus — and perhaps in all of Augustan poetry — is the definition of art in *An Essay on Criticism* (1711):

> *True Wit* is *Nature* to Advantage drest,
> What oft was *Thought*, but ne'er so well *Exprest*.[1]
>
> (297–8)

These lines have been taken as the central statement of neo-classical aesthetics, and for that reason they have been subtly read and reread by modern critics seeking to define precisely the delicate interaction between art and nature that Pope's metaphor implies. Reuben Brower, in a sustained analysis of Pope's use of the terms wit and nature, suggests that:

> when Pope says, 'True Wit is Nature to advantage dressed,' it is clear that he means much more by Nature than commonplace knowledge. To know nature is to know a good deal; 'to dress Nature to advantage' means to bring out the order and grace, the life and the surprising irregularity that only true poets can see. . . . he is not saying that poetry gives us platitudes pleasantly served up in fancy dress. . . . [nor does he regard] diction or style as a superficial adornment of thought.[2]

For Edward Niles Hooker:

> To define wit . . . as 'What oft was thought, but ne'er
> so well expressed,' does not say or imply that wit is a
> stale or commonplace thought nicely tricked out. The
> definition rather supposes that the writer, starting
> with a common and universal experience, sees it in a
> new light; and his sensitive spirit, endowing it with
> life and fresh meaning, provides it with form, image,
> language, and harmony appropriate to it. It pre-
> supposes the liveliness and insight of the creative
> mind; and it demands propriety, the perfect agree-
> ment of words, thoughts (as reshaped by the artist),
> and subject. The result is nature, and it is wit.[3]

Patricia Meyer Spacks reads the image as that of 'the
painter skilled enough to dress [nature] properly — "to
Advantage" ' — as opposed to the mere decorator, whose
false wit obscures rather than reveals Pope's notion of this
'living Grace' (294).[4]

The references to false wit, to propriety, insight, knowledge, grace and true poetry in these explications of Pope's
aesthetic reveal its ethical side — an ethics often un-
critically celebrated by modern students of the period.
Thomas R. Edwards, for example, takes as the opening
premise of his reading of Pope's poetry 'that Pope seems to
me a moral poet, just as he professed to be, and that his
morality provides one of the most impressive statements in
literature of what it means to be human.'[5] Martin Price
argues that Pope's satires move increasingly toward 'an art
that goes beyond mere beauty and weds its aesthetic
power to moral vision.'[6] And Paul Fussell, in his influential
description of 'the rhetorical world of Augustan humanism',
admires the 'moral beauty' of an aesthetic vision like
Pope's. For Fussell, Pope's art is at once a mode of representation and an act of adjudication through which an
elaborate and sophisticated linguistic structure, emulative
of the imperial age of Roman culture, shapes a 'world'
where rhetoric, belief and morality perfectly intersect.[7]

We can hardly go wrong, then, if we take this couplet as our opening paradigm. Its juxtaposition of the object of mimesis and the transforming effect of art reflects a crucial tension which we shall have occasion to explore in our discussion of *The Rape of the Lock*. What exactly does 'True Wit' do to 'Nature' to make it more natural, more beautiful, more reflective of our thoughts? Indeed, this same question of the construction of 'Nature' by 'Wit', a question that we might describe as a grounding mystification in Pope's aesthetics, arises not only in abstract formulations like the one from the *Essay on Criticism*, but also repeatedly in Pope's poetic practice. *Windsor-Forest*, for example, claims to render a balanced pastoral landscape, but, as we shall see in our examination of the Eden scenes of that poem, Pope's 'Nature' is not the landscape of England at all but a naturalized fantasy about English culture, a production of 'True Wit' with a very specific political significance. In other words, Pope's famous couplet on 'True Wit' outlines an essential problem that is also present in the larger structures of a variety of poems throughout his career. It is this problem, and the numerous interconnected contradictions which it entails, that we shall begin to explore in Pope's early works.

I

If the *Essay on Criticism* illustrates the most abstract version of the neo-classical metaphor of art as 'dress', *The Rape of the Lock* (1712, 1714, 1717) gives that metaphor substance in the form of a well-dressed eighteenth-century lady. In fact the same problematic interaction between art and nature characterizes the definition of Belinda's beauty in the famous toilet scene from Canto I of *The Rape of the Lock*:

> Now awful Beauty puts on all its Arms;
> The Fair each moment rises in her Charms,

Repairs her Smiles, awakens ev'ry Grace,
And calls forth all the Wonders of her Face;
Sees by Degrees a purer Blush arise,
And keener Lightnings quicken in her Eyes.

(I, 139—44)

Is Belinda naturally beautiful, or is it the art of the 'Cosmetic Pow'rs' (124) that makes her so? The passage seems to suggest both: that Belinda is only 'awakening' or 'calling forth' the 'awful Beauty' already latent in the 'heav'nly Image' (125) that she worships in the mirror, but also that her efforts confer a 'purer' or a 'keener' loveliness than the merely pure or keen qualities of the unadorned original. Belinda is dressed — or rather made up — to advantage here, with the same ambivalence as that of Pope's aesthetic prescription. But her beauty, unlike the abstract 'True Wit' of the *Essay on Criticism*, has a specific source. She is 'deck'd with all that Land and Sea afford' (V, 11):

Unnumber'd Treasures ope at once, and here
The various Off'rings of the World appear;
From each she nicely culls with curious Toil,
And decks the Goddess with the glitt'ring Spoil.
This Casket *India*'s glowing Gems unlocks,
And all *Arabia* breathes from yonder Box.
The Tortoise here and Elephant unite,
Transformed to *Combs*, the speckled and the white.
Here Files of Pins extend their shining Rows,
Puffs, Powders, Patches, Bibles, Billet-doux.

(I, 129—38)

Belinda is adorned with the spoils of mercantile expansion: the gems of India, the perfumes of Arabia, tortoiseshell and ivory from Africa — these are the means by which her natural beauty is 'awakened'.[8] In other words, imperialism dresses nature to advantage here; the allusion to imperial expansion in *The Rape of the Lock* makes concrete the metaphor for the operations of 'True Wit' in the *Essay on Criticism*.

The representation of the products of mercantilism in this passage not only confers a special sort of beauty upon Belinda, it also generates a special kind of rhetoric: these lines illustrate two distinctive and related formal structures that we shall find repeated, revised and played upon throughout Pope's major poetry. First, the imperial 'spoils' are laid out in an imitation of a natural scene. The verbs, especially 'extend' and 'appear', reproduce the typical predication of Pope's pastoral description. They are static, pictorial terms designed to locate objects in a framed setting. Similarly, the repeated indications of specific location — 'this' and 'yonder', 'here' and 'here' — also typical of Pope's pastorals, imitate verbally the representation of foreground and background in a landscape painting.[9] Second, the objects represented in this pseudo-landscape take over the scene; the verbs and adverbs that we have just noticed are mere gestures, serving to point out the 'glittering', 'glowing', 'breathing', 'shining' items that occupy the centre of sensual attention. These objects, then, are rhetorically foregrounded, even though semantically the passage places some 'here' and some 'yonder', in the background. In fact, where they are actually said to stand is irrelevant; they are 'innumerable', they shine and glow everywhere with an indiscriminate profusion. This indiscriminacy is essential to the scene's effect.

The last line — 'Puffs, Powders, Patches, Bibles, Billet-doux' — compactly summarizes the impression of arbitrary accumulation that dominates the whole passage. But despite this air of indiscriminacy, the list is carefully structured in sound and rhythm: it progresses from one- to two- to three-syllable units with a systematically cumulative effect, and the units are connected by the alliteration of the phonetically parallel plosives 'p' and 'b', which lead the reader's ear through the line. The final foreign word 'Billet-doux' — already typically made English by its second-position rhyme with 'Rows' — is even more insistently levelled through its smooth incorporation into the phonetic and metrical coherence of the line, as if real linguistic differences can readily be erased by the euphonious art of the heroic couplet. This powerful phonetic connection of words stands in diametrical opposition to the random relationship of things in the passage. The list does not distinguish 'Bibles' from 'Billet-doux', a failure that in this poem indicates an implicit moral irresponsibility or disorder operating in contradiction to the poetic order of the line.

Pope may have learned this listing rhetoric from Milton's 'Rocks, caves, lakes, fens, bogs, dens, and shades of death'.[10] But his use of it clearly belongs to a contemporary discourse of mercantile expansion. In 1718 J. Jocelyn defended the activities of the East India Company by enumerating the 'Commodities' — in particular those for female consumption — that the trade with the East brought home to England: '*Salt-Petre, Indigo, Muslins, Cotton-Yarn, Cotton-Wool, Ereny-Yarn, Floretta-Yarn, Herba Taffaties, Herba Longees and Callicoes*, besides *Diamonds, Drugs and Spices*'.[11] And *The Antiquity and Honourableness of the Practice of Merchandize* (1744), a mercantilist sermon of the period, compares England to the biblical trade centre of Tyre, where 'fleets brought . . . all the useful and rare commodities of the then known world . . . silver, iron, tin, lead, brass, slaves, horses, mules, ivory, ebony, emeralds, purple, embroidery, fine linen, coral, wheat, pannag [balsam], honey, oil, balm, wine, white wool, bright iron [steel], cassia, calamus, precious cloaths, lambs, rams, goats, spices, precious stones, gold, blue cloaths and rich apparel.'[12] The pure multiplication of terms characteristic of these lists is identical to Pope's representation of arbitrary proliferation. And they also reproduce in prose the phonetic and rhythmic associations of Pope's heroic couplets, without the irony or conscious artistry. The repetitions of 'cotton', 'yarn' and 'herba' in the first list link the items verbally, and the alliterative 'd' at the end of the passage provides the same kind of phonetic logic for the last section of the catalogue. In the second list a symptomatic illogic becomes evident when raw materials, precious metals, jewels, processed products, livestock and human beings are thrown together without discrimination, except that of euphonious language. Alliteration, assonance, rhyme or identical rhythm run through the passage, joining 'ivory' and 'ebony'; 'ebony' and 'emeralds'; 'linen' and 'coral'; 'oil' and 'balm'; 'wine' and 'white wool'; 'white wool' and 'bright iron'; 'cassia', 'calamus' and 'precious cloaths'; 'lambs' and 'rams'; 'spices' and 'precious stones'. These phonetic connections naturalize the representation of accumulation, providing a verbal justification for the ruthless heaping up of objects that have lost their distinctiveness from one another in their numerousness. This is the rhetoric of acquisition. In each of these catalogues the simple list of goods carries a raw and inherent fascination, an effect that is caught and heightened in Pope's passage by the collective visual attractiveness of the items and the wit that holds them together.

Pope is joining in a mercantilist discourse whose currency is widespread not only in the prose accounts of imperialism, but in the poetry as well. The year before the publication of the 1714 version of *The Rape of the Lock*, Thomas Tickell gathered the same themes into a parallel passage:

> Fearless our merchant now pursues his gain,
> And roams securely o'er the boundless main.
> Now o'er his head the polar Bear he spies,
> And freezing spangles of the Lapland skies;
> Now swells his canvas to the sultry line,
> With glittering spoils where Indian grottos shine.
> Where fumes of incense glad the southern seas,
> And wafted citron scents the balmy breeze.[13]

Though Pope may have picked up his 'glitt'ring Spoil' from Tickell, the general mercantilist sentiment is a separate but parallel growth. Pope wrote a similar passage, which we shall shortly examine, in *Windsor-Forest* before he knew of Tickell's poem.[14] Richard Blackmore's *Creation* (1712) comes even closer to Pope's list of commodities:

Ye *Britons*, who the Fruit of Commerce find,
How is your Isle a Debtor to the Wind,
Which thither wafts *Arabia*'s fragrant Spoils,
Gemms, Pearls and Spices from the *Indian* Isles,
From *Persia* Silks, Wines from *Iberia*'s Shore,
Peruvian Drugs, and *Guinea*'s Golden Oar?
Delights and Wealth to fair *Augusta* flow
From ev'ry Region whence the Winds can blow.[15]

We need not be surprised by the coincidence; *The Rape of the Lock* is built upon some of the central images of a prominent contemporary vision. Even the poem's recurrent references to tea, coffee and chocolate locate it in a mercantilist context. According to Defoe's *Review*, 'Coffee, *Tea*, and *Chocolate* ... it is well known are now become the Capital Branches of the Nations Commerce.'[16] But Pope is shaping and commenting upon that contemporary vision in his own manner. For Belinda, mercantilism is beauty. In this dressing scene, the poem identifies her in terms of the products of mercantilist expansion, and it begins to develop a rhetoric of the commodity through which she and her culture can be described − a language of commodity fetishism where objects become the only reality.[17]

The Marxian concept of the fetishism of the commodity is particularly useful here, because it binds the formal features of Pope's text to the historical facts of the im- mediate context. Fetishism is a consequence of the extension and generalization of commodity exchange, phenomena fundamentally linked in early eighteenth- century England to mercantile expansion. Commodity fetishism refers to the tendency for relations between people to be mediated by and thus to be seen as relations between things, the tendency, that is, for exchange value to be taken as the defining category in all relationships. When products acquire their value not from their utility, but by being exchanged for other products, every object comes to be viewed not in itself but in terms of those other objects.[18] This kind of equivalence, by which everything is defined through the uniform valuation of the commodity market, makes objects mutually interchangeable, indiscriminate despite their desirability, like the spoils of Pope's commodity catalogue. The result is a world in which objects have taken over all meaning. Belinda's beauty can only be seen through the commodities that she wears; the question of whether there is a real beauty, or a real Belinda, behind those spoils remains unanswered. What is equally obscured in Pope's imperialist poems is the actual production of the commodities so glowingly evoked, the labour that is necessarily exploited overseas in order to acquire these commercial spoils. Such an exclusion of the human is characteristic both of mercantile imperialism and of commodity fetishism: in the one because labour is located in a distant land, in the other because the objects stand in for the people who produce them. Indeed we might even say that the invisibility of the human producers of Belinda's spoils is symbolically avenged upon Belinda and the other human beneficiaries of that exploitation, who are themselves in turn excluded from representation in their own poems, except as versions of the objects they acquire.

The contemporary fantasy — sometimes known as Whig panegyric — that we have been examining in Blackmore, Tickell and Pope has a concrete historical motivation — the first major era of modern English imperial expansion. Imperialism has arisen in conjunction with a variety of modes of production. In the broadest sense it can be defined as the military, political or economic domination of one country by another — a domination, though, that does not necessarily entail direct colonial control. As George Lichtheim says:

> The only thing that matters to those concerned is the actual possession or loss of their freedom. If a country is invaded by a stronger power and its political institutions are destroyed or remolded, that country

is under imperial domination, whatever the political circumstances of the case, and whether or not the whole transaction is classifiable as 'progressive' or 'reactionary,' according to some canon of historical interpretation. Likewise, sovereignty may be infringed by diplomatic means, by treaty, or by economic pressure. A backward country legally prevented from developing its industries suffers a loss of sovereignty no less real because it may be invisible to the naked eye of the beholder. What counts is the relationship of domination and subjection, which is the essence of every imperial regime.[19]

English imperialism did not begin in the eighteenth century; its commercial component is significant in the English economy from at least 1650. But especially after 1713, imperialism undergoes a rapid expansion and an increasing orientation toward the trade or commercially based version that serves the interests of a pre-industrial capitalist society. Neatly enough, this first period of major growth ends perhaps as early as 1748, around the time of Pope's death, and certainly no later than the last quarter of the eighteenth century, with the Industrial Revolution, the American Revolution and the beginning of a new imperialist era. The period of Pope's major poetic production thus coincides closely with what Christopher Hill has called England's first empire, a mercantile system characterized by a national policy of protectionism, concern for favourable balance and terms of trade, coercive control over colonial production and commerce, accumulation of precious metals, support for domestic industry, and hostility towards the other major imperial powers — Holland and later France. The wars of this period are for England all commercial struggles, even when they seem to have the traditional guise of a contest for land. And England emerged from these trade wars as the dominant commercial power in the extra-European world. Indeed, after 1713 London was the centre of world commerce. By that time at least a quarter of its population was directly involved in the port trades, with most of the rest providing an infrastructure. No wonder trade and the praise of trade seem to have been on everyone's lips.[20]

The English imperial system of this period had its focus in India and the Atlantic. The first Dutch war of 1652—4 had opened the Far East to English trade, and by 1700 the East India Company was realizing huge profits from the area. In return for silver bullion exported to the East, the Company received much greater value in textile raw materials — silk, linen and cotton — and by the mid-eighteenth century in tea as well. Settled in fortified trading centres, by the late seventeenth century the Company had begun making plans to tax the population that its fortifications were designed to control. By the early eighteenth century the East India Company was England's biggest business, laying the foundation for the future colonial empire in India that began to take shape shortly after Pope's death; its profits may well have been important in spurring the Industrial Revolution. In the century after 1650 England also established a multi-lateral Atlantic economy linking the British Isles to Africa, the Caribbean and North America. English traders bought slaves in Africa, sold them in the West Indies, and returned to England with the sugar of the Caribbean slave plantations. This was the Triangle Trade, into which the American colonies were gradually integrated as an ultimately essential fourth stop. The growth of this system in the eighteenth century, and particularly of the slave trade, was a crucial source of English prosperity. The victims, of course, were overwhelmingly the slaves themselves, but after 1720 the North American colonies suffered as well from restrictions on industrial production and commerce.[21]

The Peace of Utrecht of 1713, concluding the War of the Spanish Succession with France, intensified and in some cases codified these trends. By its provisions England received Newfoundland, Nova Scotia, the Hudson Bay Territories, Fort James in Senegambia, Gibraltar and

Minorca. It also attained equality with France in trade with Spain and supplanted France in holding the Asiento grant, a monopoly contract to supply 4,800 slaves a year to the Spanish New World. As a result of these gains, England replaced Holland as the major European slave-trading nation. After 1730 Parliament provided financial support for forts on the Gold Coast to protect the interests of the slave traders. The rise of free trade acted as a spur to trade in slaves; the weakening of the Royal African Company's monopoly on the slave trade in 1698, and the elimination of all restriction on competitors in 1712, resulted in an even higher volume of slave traffic. Annual exportation estimates for the boom years after 1713 range from 40,000 to 100,000. The South Sea Company, the main beneficiary of the end of monopoly, produced an even higher mortality rate in its slave transport ships than the Royal African Company. Yet even death rates as high as 20 per cent posed little problem to entrepreneurs who could sell their cargo to Caribbean plantations at five times their cost. Ninety per cent of plantation capital, excluding land, went into the purchase of slaves, largely because those purchased did not last long; the average life expectancy of a slave entering a West Indian plantation was no more than ten years.[22]

A similar if less extreme pattern characterized the development of the southern colonies of British North America. After 1713 tobacco production in Virginia and Maryland was increasingly taken over by large slave planta-tions; rice production in South Carolina followed the same route. The slave population of the southern colonies increased from no more than 25,000 in 1700 to over 300,000 in the 1770s, one quarter of the total population of the region. Slaves had little economic importance in New England and the middle Atlantic colonies, but Rhode Island became a centre of the slave trade, and the other northern colonies entered into close trade relations with the slave economies of the West Indies. At the same time, these colonies engaged in intermittent conflict with the native American Indians, whose land they gradually expropriated.[23]

So far, we have raised the issue of capitalism and the context of England's first mercantile empire by extrapolating from the description of the 'spoils' with which Belinda is dressed. But we have had to labour somewhat to uncover those allusions. *The Rape of the Lock* does not present itself immediately as a poem about imperialism or the fetishism of the commodity. On the contrary, many readers would say that the poem specifically denies or transcends such issues. Critics of *The Rape of the Lock* have typically discovered two separate ways of assessing Pope's attitude toward Belinda. Most find a preponderance of satire and see the poem as an ironic critique of Belinda and her world from a variety of directions. But many readers also see the work, at least in part, as a flattering, fascinated appreciation.[24] There seems to be a kind of double vision in the structure of this poem that makes both of these readings possible. Perhaps if we can see how they function together we can begin to understand something more of the relevance of imperialist ideology to Pope's poetic form.

We have already glimpsed, on the one hand, an implicit attack on Belinda through her association with the anarchic commodities of the toilet scene. The deflating irony of 'Puffs, Powders, Patches, Bibles, Billet-doux' recurs throughout the poem in reference to the values of Belinda's world. Thalestris's speech in Canto IV, for instance, contains the same anarchic catalogue:

> Sooner let Earth, Air, Sea, to *Chaos* fall,
> Men, Monkies, Lap-dogs, Parrots, perish all!
>
> (IV, 119–20)

This typical failure of discrimination is most frequently represented through zeugma — the use of a single verb to level disparate subjects or objects — the poem's most distinctive rhetorical device. Here the verbs 'break', 'stain', 'forget' and 'lose' conflate serious and trivial accidents:

Whether the Nymph shall break *Diana*'s Law,
Or some frail *China* Jar receive a Flaw,
Or stain her Honour, or her new Brocade,
Forget her Pray'rs, or miss a Masquerade,
Or lose her Heart, or Necklace, at a Ball;
Or whether Heav'n has doom'd that *Shock* must fall.

(II, 105—10)

Major political events are verbally indistinguishable from trivial private affairs:

Here *Britain*'s Statesmen oft the Fall foredoom
Of Foreign Tyrants, and of Nymphs at home;
Here Thou, Great *Anna*! whom three Realms obey,
Dost sometimes Counsel take — and sometimes *Tea*.

(III, 5—8)

And mortality, in this passage and elsewhere, is reduced to a casual catch-all — husbands and lap-dogs, men and monkeys:

Not louder Shrieks to pitying Heav'n are cast,
When Husbands or when Lap-dogs breathe their last.

(III, 157—58)

Triviality, moral anarchy, insignificance — these judgements are already implicit even in the title of the poem, 'the rape of the lock', with its confusion of the practical joke of the snipping of Belinda's lock with sexual violation; they are programmatically recorded in the rhetorical structure of the work; and they are typically linked to the language of commodity fetishism by which Belinda is initially defined.

Pope also trivializes Belinda through the ironic juxtaposition of her story with classical epic. The poem's title not only conflates momentous with insignificant sexual acts, it also juxtaposes a heroic classical theme with a modern prank. It alludes, of course, to the *Iliad*, contrasting the abduction of Helen with an insignificant social squabble. Heroic material, primarily from the *Iliad* and

Aeneid but also from *Paradise Lost*, dominates the language and major themes of the work. Belinda's card game in Canto III and her quarrel with the Baron in Canto V are both recounted in the terms of heroic battle. The Sylphs serve in place of the gods as epic machinery, directing mortal affairs. The poem opens with a proper invocation to the Muse, contains a trip to the underworld like those undertaken by Odysseus and Aeneas, and echoes in detail passages from the classics, the lengthiest being the speech of Sarpedon to Glaucus from Book XII of the *Iliad*, which Pope had translated earlier and which forms the basis of Clarissa's speech in Canto V. This heroic material serves in one respect to make a mockery of Belinda. Her trivial, commodified and amoral world is contrasted with the grandeur of epic, a world of gods and goddesses, of heroes larger than life, where history is made and great nations find their identity. Thus Belinda's world of things is shown to be essentially incompatible with the world of heroism. Heroes don't own commodities; this is the primary formal configuration of the poem.

Belinda is not only trivialized and deflated, however, and the mock-heroic structure of the poem does not work only to set the heroic against the contemporary world. We have already had a glimpse of this other side of the poem's coin in our discussion of the seductiveness of accumulation as it is represented in the commodity catalogue. The very language that trivializes Belinda makes her fascinating and attractive too. And similarly, the heroic material also moves both ways, deflating Belinda and at the same time giving her the stature of a goddess and her story the status of an epic. The climactic apotheosis of Belinda's lock at the end of the poem can of course be read as a joke, but it can also be read — especially to the extent that it represents Pope's poetic consecration of her lock to fame — as a real apotheosis for the poem, for Belinda, and for the new, more visually dazzling heroics of contemporary England. On the one hand, *The Rape of the Lock* seems to imply that the age of heroism is lost forever to the modern world and thus can serve only as an ironic reminder of our present reduced state. On the other hand, the poem seems to move towards epic, suggesting that — at least in some respect — contemporary English culture does resemble the great age of Rome. This movement between ironic distance and celebratory proximity is typical of Pope's use of epic allusion, here and throughout his corpus.

We have thus far taken Pope at his word. That is, we have examined primarily those effects that he deliberately seeks to create in *The Rape of the Lock*. And those effects are certainly complex enough: a character and context that are both ridiculed and admired, a mock-heroic discrepancy that becomes a problematic equation. But what remains to be discovered in *The Rape of the Lock* is the ideological significance of this complicated structure. What does it mean for an expanding mercantilist culture to be construed as both like and unlike the heroic age of Virgil?

To the extent that it is unlike, that the use of heroic allusion is ironic, the poem claims an absolute disjunction between commodification and classical heroism. Belinda is no goddess. She is a modern lady decked out with the things of contemporary culture. Rome had no such trivial concerns. To the extent that the epic material elevates and celebrates Belinda's world, the poem claims that the incipient English empire is a modern version of the great age of Rome, fighting the same grand battles, and creating an equivalent cultural edifice; the two imperial missions are the same. From this perspective, Belinda's spoils are not amoral commodities but the glowing emblems of that mission. As this period well knew, however, the story of imperial conquest recounted in classical epic entailed the enrichment of Roman culture through the accumulation of products from all over the Mediterranean. Imperial Rome is the great pre-modern centre of the commodity; the satires of Juvenal provide just one testimony to that fact. But it is precisely this equation of Roman and English history that Pope seems determined to conceal. The attractions of Belinda's society are presented in terms of classical allusion, but its failings are all seen as fallings away from the heroic. The resultant segmentation, by which Belinda's world of things is separated off from any connection with classical epic, enables the poem to avoid the implication that imperialism produces a fetishism of the commodity, a moral anarchy and degradation of culture. The poem can thus attack commodities and their cultural consequences while it extols imperialism. It can praise the battles of imperial expansion while it condemns the consequences of capitalist accumulation. We shall see the same strange formal dichotomy at the end of Pope's career, in *The Dunciad*.

But *The Rape of the Lock*'s attempt at falsification supplies its greatest insight. Through its own complicated evasions of the conjunctions of imperialism and commodification, it produces a structure that serves in the end to reveal that conjunction. First of all, by making the commodity its god (or goddess) in the person of Belinda, the poem admits its unconscious obsession with the connection of classical imperialist ideology and commodity fetishism. And furthermore, if Belinda stands for the products of mercantilism, her story in turn enacts the violence of imperial war. Battles dominate Cantos III and V; and war pervades the poem, beginning when Belinda 'arms' herself in the toilet scene of Canto I and ending only with the 'Millions slain' (146) of the last verse paragraph. Of all the major works of its period, *The Rape of the Lock* does the most to match imperialism and commodity fetishism, and the most to place the commodification of English culture in the context of imperial violence. The original version of the poem, like *An Essay on Criticism* and substantial parts of *Windsor-Forest*, was composed during the major imperial war of the first part of the eighteenth century, the War of the Spanish Succession. It was a controversial and bloody conflict, fought nominally to prevent French succession to the Spanish throne, but actually and relatedly to keep France — England's major imperial rival — from possessing itself of all the territories and trading monopolies of the old Spanish empire. As we have seen, England's victory, negotiated at the Peace of Utrecht, represented the first stage of the establishment of English mercantile supremacy in the New World.

It is not surprising, then, that *The Rape of the Lock* seems, almost despite itself, to be obsessed with imperialism and its consequences for English culture. Nor is it unusual that in this period of imperial expansion Pope and others should select Augustan Rome as a cultural model, albeit necessarily a problematic one. The neo-classical movement finds it apotheosis and its coda in this convergence of imperialist ideologies: never before was classicism so deeply in tune with the dynamic ideological structures of English literature, and never again would it play the same role in enabling and elaborating the primary expressions of English culture. What we have seen of classical allusion in *The Rape of the Lock* can indicate the complexity of this role. The neo-classical material in Pope's poem in part simply gives prestige to the notion of empire; to the extent that the contemporary English are like the heroic Romans, their national project must be as valuable as the construction of the Roman empire. But our description of the poem's structure indicates that the classical material actually enables Pope to produce a special sort of statement about English culture — a statement that recognizes the destructive cultural effects of commodification while maintaining allegiance to the imperialist ideology which produces those effects. In other words, without neo-classicism Pope could not have produced his complex rationalization of imperialism. The classical material upon which he draws is not merely a passive repository, but rather an active agent in shaping and shoring up his central fantasies about his society.

Perhaps the best indication of the active and reciprocal relation between Pope's poems and their classical materials is Pope's use of the *Iliad* in *The Rape of the Lock*. As we have already seen, thematic allusions to classical epic are pervasive in the poem. Verbal echoes tend to refer predominantly to Dryden's translation of the *Aeneid* — the period's most influential redaction of the classics — or to Pope's own contemporary translation of the *Iliad*. The relationship of Pope's poem to Pope's translation is strangely unstraightforward, however. *The Rape of the Lock* was published first in three books in 1712, and then in five books in 1714, substantially as we have it now; later, in 1717, Pope added Clarissa's speech in Canto V. Pope's translation of the *Iliad* began appearing in 1715, and was finally complete in 1726. We have some evidence that he began his translation in early 1714, around the time (late 1713, presumably) when he was completing his revisions of *The Rape of the Lock*. The timing is crucial, because it indicates that at several points the earlier *Rape of the Lock* contains passages that Pope later included in his *Iliad* translation in a way that makes Homer seem to echo Pope. William Frost has shown that in at least one couplet in both the 1712 and the 1714 versions of *The Rape of the Lock*, Pope 'alludes' directly to a couplet from Book XX of his *Iliad*, which was not translated until 1718:[25]

When those fair Suns shall sett, as sett they must,
And all those Tresses shall be laid in Dust.
(*The Rape of the Lock*, V, 147–8)

But when the Day decreed (for come it must)
Shall lay this dreadful Hero in the Dust.
(*Iliad*, XX, 385–6)

This translation, in short, was written in imitation of *The Rape of the Lock*. In several other cases, as Frost suggests, the influence of *The Rape of the Lock* on the *Iliad* is likely, but more difficult to prove. The first part of the Baron's oath in Book IV (133–6) seems to anticipate Achilles' oath in Book I of the *Iliad*, though the resemblance may be derived from a third source. The couplet, 'Where Wigs with Wigs, with Sword-knots Sword-knots

strive,/Beaus banish Beaus, and Coaches Coaches drive'
(I, 101—2), resembles similar synecdochic battle scenes in
Books IV (1715) and XIII (1717) of Pope's *Iliad*, but since
this is a common rhetorical device in heroic poetry, it may
not necessarily have a specific connection with *The Rape
of the Lock*. The line from the toilet scene — 'And *Betty*'s
prais'd for Labours not her own' (I, 148) — echoes *Iliad*
Book II (1715) — 'And *Troy* prevails by Armies not her
own' (160). In this case it is possible that *The Rape of the
Lock* influenced the *Iliad*, but also possible that the two
couplets were composed simultaneously during the brief
period in 1713—14 when Pope may have been working on
both poems at once. If the latter is the case, the modern
mock-heroic and the classical 'original' could be said to be
contemporaries.

   In a sense Pope's interest in his own verse is predictable,
and self-reference, as we shall see, is common throughout
Pope's corpus. In another respect, however, Pope is
creating his neo-classical models out of his own poetry. He
is both imitating the classics and making the classics
imitate him in a reciprocal move reminiscent of Belinda's
creation of herself as a goddess in the toilet scene with
which we began. William Warburton, Pope's earliest editor,
criticized this scene for confusing Belinda's role: he com-
plained that Belinda is described at one moment as the
goddess herself and at the next as the high priestess who
worships and adorns that goddess.[26] Our examination of
Pope's use of Homer should show us that the poet was not
simply inattentive here. Belinda's vision of herself in the
mirror and the resulting reversibility of creating subject
and aesthetic object, of poet and nature, in fact enact the
ideological strategy of the whole poem. In the same way,
Pope's classical allusions reflect not an objective, extrinsic,
ancient authority, but a mirror-image of the poet's own
words, of *The Rape of the Lock* itself. The notion of an
originary classical model, like that of an originary nature
or beauty for Belinda, becomes characteristically problematic. The elaborate ideological structures of the poem,

then, its elegant fantasy about modern English culture, represents an act of reciprocal self-construction in which the subjective is seen as objective and thereby justified and naturalized. In other words, Pope makes a classical 'past' out of his own present beliefs. But that past does not become entirely Pope's. It partly explains and elaborates his beliefs and partly generates them, in the sense that it is only through the classics that *The Rape of the Lock* can fully imagine the fantasy that it embodies. The 'real' classics can regain some autonomy in this context, and in the process Pope's use of them becomes even more complex. If what Pope gives us is Homer or Virgil according to their utility in his ideological system, then we might suspect that what Pope would most want to neglect in his rewriting of classical epic is its ambivalent relationship to the cultural consequences of national expansion.

Recent readings, especially of the *Aeneid*, have indeed suggested that that poem's representation of the ideology of empire is deeply fissured. The role of Aeneas, for example, is at least two-sided. The incompatibility between his pious ideals and his ineffectual or even reprehensible actions seems to call into question the coherence and plausibility of Augustan heroism. Relatedly, the poem appears at least partially pessimistic in its treatment of the image of the Augustan peace. And Virgil's attitude towards Augustus himself, if we can extrapolate from the poem, may well be more ambivalent than a reading that emphasizes the straightforward celebration of empire would suggest. To the extent that the *Aeneid* promises heroism, harmony and historical triumph, it often fails to fulfil those promises. W.R. Johnson summarizes one aspect of this view as follows: 'In respect of intellectual climate, then, it is possible to see in Vergil's time not an age of faith but the beginning of the age of anxiety.'[27] If this is true, we might even rephrase our formulation. Perhaps the *Aeneid*'s own ambivalences, in addition to the more obvious apology for imperialism, underlie Pope's fascination with the classics: though Pope explicitly uses Virgil as a model and justification for an imperialist culture, Virgil's very ambiguities may attract a poet whose works contain similar tensions. We could even speculate that the contradictions in the *Aeneid* serve as a model of another kind, a subliminal and subversive one, for the implicit ambivalence of Pope's imperialist poems.

The reciprocal gesture that we have identified in this poem's neo-classicism can serve as a useful model for our definition of ideology — a central concern in our reading of Pope. The image of the mirror in the toilet scene and the merging of subject and object that we noted both there and in Pope's classical allusions illustrate a typical aspect of ideology formation. The subject constructs reality out of itself; it sees the world in its own image and records that image as external. Its connection with contemporary reality, then, lies not in the image that it sees, like Belinda, in the mirror, but rather in the pressures it feels to construct itself as it does, in the gaps it needs to fill, the conclusions it must conceal, the tensions it attempts to relieve, and the contradictions it is determined to resolve.

The notion of neo-classicism as an invented memory with an ideological end, which we have developed from our reading of *The Rape of the Lock*, is very different from the treatment that Pope's use of classical allusion typically receives. Such a reading provides a way of defining what the neo-classical movement means in its historical context. Indeed classicism, despite its antiquarian cast, gives us a special leverage upon the present: the more we know about Pope's use of the classics, the more we can understand about the system of beliefs that justified English imperial expansion at almost its tenderest age. Our perspective can also enable us to understand sentiments like Reuben Brower's in his important book on Pope's classicism. Quoting G.M. Trevelyan, Brower commends Pope's ability, through his use of the classics, to represent in all its glory 'the greatness of England' in this age of expansion.[28] We need not share this valorization of English imperialism to read Pope; in fact we must not, if we expect to be able to grasp the most subtle and in a sense the most artful structures of his neo-classical form.

II

In *Windsor-Forest* the rhetoric of commodity fetishism that we identified only briefly and locally in *The Rape of the Lock* comes into its own. The two poems describe the effects of mercantile expansion in very similar ways, but *Windsor-Forest*, unlike *The Rape of the Lock*, makes that problem its central thesis. Indeed, Pope's career is framed by the two major works that directly address the issue of the English nation: *Windsor-Forest* and *The Dunciad*. Both are apocalyptic poems, bearing witness to the coming of a new era in English culture, though they see that apocalypse from opposing perspectives. The comparison of *Windsor-Forest* and *The Rape of the Lock* should give us an opportunity to define the formal structures most typical of Pope's representation of the 'great age' of English imperialism at this early moment in his career. But we shall ultimately need to ask where those structures lead and what the rhetoric of commodity fetishism means at the other pole of Pope's career in *The Dunciad*.

We began our discussion of *The Rape of the Lock* with the treasures of Belinda's dressing table. Those same treasures appear in the opening and closing passages of *Windsor-Forest*, where the poem most explicitly celebrates the expanded trading monopolies negotiated at the Peace of Utrecht:

> Let *India* boast her Plants, nor envy we
> The weeping Amber or the balmy Tree,
> While by our Oaks the precious Loads are born,
> And Realms commanded which those Trees adorn.
>
> (29–32)

For me the Balm shall bleed, and Amber flow,
The Coral redden, and the Ruby glow,
The Pearly Shell its lucid Globe infold,
And *Phoebus* warm the ripening Ore to Gold.
(393—6)

These are commodity catalogues of the same sort and even
containing the same goods that we encountered in *The
Rape of the Lock*. Again, they are characterized by
descriptive profusion, colour, light and an indiscriminate
glowing vista of products. Here, though, we find the simple
listing rhetoric of Belinda's toilet linked to and elaborated
by a rhetorical device less prominent in *The Rape of the
Lock* but centrally exploited in *Windsor-Forest*: a
systematic substitution of a part for the whole, or synecdoche. In *The Rape of the Lock* when Ariel describes the
epic battles within the 'moving Toyshop' of the female
heart, he dismembers the combatant heroes, representing
them through their accoutrements:

Where Wigs with Wigs, with Sword-knots Sword-knots
    strive,
Beaus banish Beaus, and Coaches Coaches drive.
(I, 101—2)

So too, in the central imperialist image of *Windsor-Forest*,
the oaks that carry the 'precious Loads' of spoils to
England are said to 'command' India, that is, the West
Indies — the main site of recent trading gains.[29] The trees
themselves, of course, command no one, except meta-
phorically: they stand for the ships of the English navy
and for the Stuart monarchy, of which the oak was the
traditional symbol. Indeed the forest synecdoche is a
poetic commonplace in the period. Thomas Tickell makes
the movement of displacement much more obvious in one
of his descriptions of the Thames, where 'a vast navy hides
his ample bed,/A floating forest'.[30] Pope's navy is both
more metaphoric and more aggressive. The synecdoche
recurs in *Windsor-Forest* as the poem comes to its climax:

Thy Trees, fair *Windsor*! now shall leave their Woods,
And half thy Forests rush into my Floods,
Bear *Britain*'s Thunder, and her Cross display,
To the bright Regions of the rising Day;
Tempt Icy Seas, where scarce the Waters roll,
Where clearer Flames glow round the frozen Pole.

(385–90)

The English navy, then, the agent of imperialism, is absent
from the poem, replaced by the picturesque pastoral image
of the oak. Its artillery is likewise present only in its sound,
translated into the natural phenomenon of thunder.

The use of synecdoche here serves to dismember the
problem of imperialism, so that it need not be confronted
as a whole, in much the same way that the commodity is
separated from the heroic in *The Rape of the Lock*.[31] But,
in addition, the dismemberment that we have seen in
Windsor-Forest consistently translates the political or
military components of English mercantilism into 'natural',
pastoral phenomena. Where *The Rape of the Lock* imitates
Homer's — or rather Pope's — *Iliad*, *Windsor* imitates
Virgil's *Georgics*. The sylvan chase that dominates the
centre of the poem opens with an allusion to the *Georgics*[32]
that summarizes in one neat simile the complicated evocation and displacement of violence typical of *Windsor-Forest*.
In this passage, characteristically, Pope makes the real issue —
imperial war — into the vehicle and uses it as an illustration
of the event at hand in the poem, the hunter netting the
feeding partridges:

Thus (if small Things we may with great compare)
When *Albion* sends her eager Sons to War,
Some thoughtless Town, with Ease and Plenty blest,
Near, and more near, the closing Lines invest;
Sudden they seize th'amaz'd, defenceless Prize,
And high in Air *Britannia*'s Standard flies.

(105–10)

The next few lines illustrate the close interaction of

pastoral description and mercantilism in the poem. The pheasant — the helpless prey of the pastoral hunter — seems to stand in for the imperial 'spoils' catalogued, as we have seen, more directly elsewhere:

> Ah! what avail his glossie, varying Dyes,
> His Purple Crest, and Scarlet-circled Eyes,
> The vivid Green his shining Plumes unfold;
> His painted Wings, and Breast that flames with Gold?
>
> (115—18)

And so do the fish, the next victims in this 'Sylvan War' (148):

> Our plenteous Streams a various Race supply;
> The bright-ey'd Perch with Fins of *Tyrian* Dye,
> The silver Eel, in shining Volumes roll'd,
> The yellow Carp, in Scales bedrop'd with Gold,
> Swift Trouts, diversify'd with Crimson Stains,
> And Pykes, the Tyrants of the watry Plains.
>
> (141—6)

The emphasis on the colour purple in the bird's crest and the 'Tyrian Dye' of the perch allude to Tyre, the biblical type of mercantile expansion and a common point of comparison in eighteenth-century celebrations of English trade, as in Edward Young's impassioned plea: 'Ply *Commerce* . . . View, emulate, outshine *Old Tyre*'.[33] These creatures constitute a list of glowing visual qualities. They are coloured — 'crimson', 'gold', 'silver', 'vivid' and 'glossie' — like the commodities in Pope's trade catalogues — the reddening coral, the glowing ruby and the ripening gold. They are, in fact, gold, silver and jewels displaced into the natural world and disguised as pastoral creatures. And they are also explicitly 'painted', decorated, dressed in these colours, as Belinda dresses herself in *The Rape of the Lock*. The similarity in language between these passages and the commodity catalogues begins to suggest how *Windsor-Forest* incorporates pastoral convention into the service of imperial power.

This incorporation is equally evident in the poem's two main moments of pastoral scene-painting, the Edenic descriptions of Windsor Forest itself. The first of these begins with a reference to Milton's Eden in Book VII of *Paradise Lost*:

> The Groves of *Eden*, vanish'd now so long,
> Live in Description, and look green in Song:
> *These*, were my Beast inspir'd with equal Flame,
> Like them in Beauty, should be like in Fame.

(7—10)

These lines introduce a long opening passage that combines the traditional identification of Windsor, King Arthur and the mythic origins of the English nation with the millennial metaphor of the peace and plenty that English trade will dispense to all the world. The pastoral landscape that forms the centrepiece of this passage contains some rhetorical effects that we have seen before:

> Here waving Groves a checquer'd Scene display,
> And part admit and part exclude the Day;
> As some coy Nymph her Lover's warm Address
> Nor quite indulges, nor can quite repress.
> There, interspers'd in Lawns and opening Glades,
> Thin Trees arise that shun each others Shades.
> Here in full Light the russet Plains extend;
> There wrapt in Clouds the blueish Hills ascend:
> Ev'n the wild Heath displays her Purple Dies,
> And 'midst the Desart fruitful Fields arise,
> That crown'd with tufted Trees and springing Corn,
> Like verdant Isles the sable Waste adorn.

(17—28)

Strangely enough, in this period even the traditional image of pastoral fertility has a mercantile valence. A contemporary encomium to commerce suggests how specifically mercantilist Pope's reference to the fruitful 'Desart' might be: '[Trade] will turn Deserts into fruitful Fields, Villages into great Cities, Cottages into Palaces.'[34] Obviously, there is more in Pope's landscape than meets the eye.

Though this is a description of a natural scene, it uses the same poetic strategy as the catalogue of commodities on Belinda's dressing table: the empty directional adverbs 'here' and 'there' move the perspective from an arbitrary foreground to an arbitrary background; the same adjectival verbs, 'extend' and 'ascend', substitute accumulation for action. But even more vividly, this passage depends on the same evocation of light and colour that we found to be central both in the commodity lists and in the related descriptions of the pheasant and the fish, suggesting the same congruence of imperial spoils and pastoral description. Again the prominent colour is the Tyrian purple of another mercantilist era; the 'verdant Isles' are like the pheasant's 'vivid green' and also like islands in a real ocean, the sea over which England's merchant navy rules. And here, too, like the fish, the pheasant and Belinda herself, the pastoral setting is dyed, painted; nature is dressed to advantage with the colours of imperialism. Colour seems to carry a special burden in these early poems — a burden closely connected with Pope's transformation of classical pastoral. This passage is in part an imitation of Homer's account of the gardens of Alcinous in the *Odyssey*, to which, as Reuben Brower has shown, Pope adds all the references to colour — a change that is even more apparent in his direct translation of that passage from Homer, where terms for colour are introduced in the absence of any equivalent in the original. Pope relatedly increases the emphasis on themes of painting, dyeing and dressing[35] — the sources of this colour and the rhetorical mechanisms by which nature is commodified both in this poem and in *The Rape of the Lock*.

The pastoral Eden of *Windsor*, then, is a commodified vision of the English state, where imperial products are translated to the English countryside in a fantasy of power that makes all the world Britain. This move involves the same kind of ideological superimposition as the one

Addison creates when he rejoices that 'whilst we enjoy the remotest Products of the North and South, we are free from those Extremities of Weather which gave them Birth; That our Eyes are refreshed with the green Fields of *Britain*, at the same time that our Palates are feasted with Fruits that rise between the Tropicks.'[36] *Windsor-Forest* sees the rural woods and hills of England and at the same time tastes the fruits of imperial exploitation in a close proximity or even simultaneity of pastoral and imperialism. It is not surprising, in this context, that the pastoral scenes in *Windsor-Forest* generate the central synecdoche of the poem. The oaks of Windsor themselves, as we have seen, bear the spoils of India to England and command the empire.

We can explore this tension further in the rhetorical structures of *Windsor*'s Eden scenes. Like Milton's Eden in *Paradise Lost*, the opening pastoral scene is characterized by proliferation, surprising fertility, discordance and, rhetorically, by oxymoron, the paradoxical verbal conjunction of opposites: 'And 'midst the Desert fruitful Fields arise ... Like verdant Isles the sable Waste adorn.' The oxymoronic structure of the scene seems to be in part generated by its excessive verdancy and colour, by its superabundant fertility and by the implicit presence of the transforming powers of trade itself. But if these oxymorons represent excess, they are rationalized in advance by the references to moderation and balance with which the passage begins: the 'checquer'd Scene' that 'part admit[s] and part exclude[s]', the 'interspers'd' lawns and glades, the lighted plains and darkened hills. These are scenic allusions to the doctrine of *concordia discors* — a classical and Renaissance notion that found implicit unity in difference, wholeness in contradiction. Pope prefaces this pastoral passage with an explicit expression of allegiance to that doctrine:

Not *Chaos*-like together crush'd and bruis'd,
But as the World, harmoniously confus'd:

Where Order in Variety we see,
And where, tho' all things differ, all agree.

(13—16)

Earl Wasserman has argued that the primary route by
which *concordia discors* was transmitted to Restoration
and eighteenth-century poetry was through John Denham's
Cooper's Hill (1642, 1655, 1668), a georgic loco-descriptive
poem with a strong direct influence on *Windsor-Forest*.[37]
Denham's famous emblematic couplet on the Thames is
certainly the best known example of *concordia discors* for
this period:

Though deep, yet clear, though gentle, yet not dull,
Strong without rage, without ore-flowing full.[38]

Denham's influence lies in his ability systematically to
instill the theme of harmonious opposition into the very
texture of his line, into the rhetoric, the rhyme and the
metrical pattern of his verse. We shall find this characteristic use of parallelism, inversion and balanced antithesis
throughout Pope's major works.

But another kind of similarity helps to explain why
Denham's prosody and its embodiment of *concordia
discors* should have been so congenial to Pope and to
Restoration and eighteenth-century heroic poetry.
Denham's Thames does not stand for just any form of
cosmic order in variety; it specifically symbolizes both a
political order in the balanced antithesis of parliamentary
monarchy and an economic order in the resultant balanced
dispersal of wealth, domestic and imperial.[39] This latter
issue is especially relevant to our reading of *Windsor-Forest*.
In *Cooper's Hill*:

No unexpected inundations spoyl
The mowers hopes, nor mock the plowmans toyl:
But God-like his [Thames'] unwearied Bounty flows;
First loves to do, then loves the Good he does:
Nor are his Blessings to his banks confin'd,
But free, and common, as the Sea or Wind;

When he to boast, or to dispense his stores
Full of the tributes of his grateful shores,
Visits the world, and in his flying towers
Brings home to us, and makes both *Indies* ours;
Finds wealth where 'tis, bestows it where it wants
Cities in deserts, woods in Cities plants.
So that to us no thing, no place is strange,
While his fair bosom is the worlds exchange.

(175–88)

Not only Denham's Thames, but his particular version of *concordia discors* and his distinctive prosody, contain a formal encoding of the paired ideologies of balanced government and mercantile prosperity central to the thinking of Pope's period. No wonder that Pope takes them over so eagerly. But we must also find it no wonder if we discover Pope's hopeful adoption of *concordia discors* to be more vexed and less seamlessly efficacious than it at first appears.

We have already seen how neo-classical allusion serves partly to justify and partly to subvert imperialist ideology in *The Rape of the Lock*. The same is true of *Windsor*'s evocation of *concordia discors*. It seeks to explain away as harmonious opposition a disturbing paradox and inversion in the pastoral setting by reference to classical precedent. But in fact it calls attention to a violation of natural order that is one of the poem's obsessions, one of its deepest formal connections to the fantastic transforming powers of mercantile imperialism, and one of the strongest specific signs of the contradictions in its ideology. The opening Eden scene is repeated, or rather mirrored, at the conclusion of the Ovidian passage midway through the poem with a different classical imitation, this time of the *Mosella* of Ausonius.[40] It arises as the climax of another scene of displaced violence — an unconsummated 'rape' like Belinda's — which includes yet another image of the helpless bird, *Windsor*'s prototypical victim of imperial power: Pan pursues Lodona like the 'fierce Eagle' does the 'trembling Doves' (185—6). Lodona in response dissolves into a silver stream which weeps to commemorate her unfortunate fate. In the glass of her tears:

> . . . the musing Shepherd spies
> The headlong Mountains and the downward Skies,
> The watry Landskip of the pendant Woods,
> And absent Trees that tremble in the Floods;
> In the clear azure Gleam the Flocks are seen,
> And floating Forests paint the Waves with Green.
>
> (211—16)

The ascending hills of the first Eden are here 'headlong'; the skies have fallen 'downward'; firmament and flood, dry land and water have lost their distinction; the trees stand trembling and inverted in the river; and the 'verdant Isles' have indeed become islands, 'floating Forests' that 'paint the Waves with Green'. The same pastoral items and the same verdancy mark this Eden, and even the painting that we have identified as an encoding of the aesthetic of imperialism in Pope's poetry recurs here. This landscape is literally overturned by oxymoron — rationalized however by the mirroring of nature in the stream rather than by *concordia discors*.

But in fact this scene only elaborates with more persistence the formal structures already present in the opening Miltonic allusion; it takes its lead from that seemingly balanced scene. There is an implicit perversion, a cataclysmic paradox, in the oxymorons of these two Edens, where chaos is unobtrusively exchanged for order, and where a peaceful logic suddenly becomes a fantastic new world. These pastoral inversions, cumulatively visible in the juxtaposition of the two oxymoronic landscapes, signal a central anxiety in *Windsor-Forest*, a tension between what seems to be represented and what lies beneath the surface. And the controlling image of this anxiety is, once again, the repressed violence of imperial war. Indeed, the sudden, seemingly magical appearance of the mystified navy is a trope of contemporary writing on imperialism. In the same passage where a personified 'Trade' turns 'Deserts into fruitful Fields', she also changes 'the Coverings of little Worms into the richest Brocades, the Fleeces of harmless Sheep into the Pride and Ornaments of Kings, and by a further Metamorphosis will transmute them again into armed Hosts and haughty Fleets.'[41] And in another contemporary comment:

> *Trade barbarous* Lands can polish fair;
> Make *Earth* well worth the *wise* Man's Care;
> Call forth her Forests, *charm* them into Fleets.[42]

In *Windsor* too, 'charmed' fleets appear fantastically from a void. Like the first Eden scene, this one contains and introduces that primary synecdoche of the poem, the 'floating Forests' of the English navy that materialize from the 'absent trees' of imperial power that grow beside the Thames:

> Thou too, great Father of the *British* Floods!
> With joyful Pride survey'st our lofty Woods,
> Where tow'ring Oaks their growing Honours rear,
> And future Navies on thy Shores appear.

> (219—22)

The 'trembling' trees are present with a vengeance in these immediately succeeding lines, where the inverted landscape, already overturned by oxymoron, now becomes an armada, and pastoral is translated to imperial, Eden to Armageddon.

The imperialist incorporation of pastoral in the sylvan battle has a similar paradoxical dimension. Like the Virgilian simile with which it begins, the hunt both conceals and reveals the violence of imperial war. In a similar manner it also ambiguously represents the suffering of the victims. That is, the displacement of the military and political into the pastoral makes an evocation of imperial oppression possible even in this celebration of the English nation. The middle scenes of this poem of peace are full of mayhem and violence. Though in his description of the sylvan creatures Pope calls the pikes 'Tyrants' who, like the opponents of English imperial expansion (here notably France), thus deserve their downfall, he gives most of the victims of this displaced violence sympathetic treatment: the partridges are pathetically 'defenceless', the pheasant is an almost tragic figure ('what avail[s]' his grandeur?). The fowler, the villain of the piece, roves the field with 'slaught'ring Guns', breaking the frozen sky with 'thunder', felling doves, 'lonely Woodcocks', lapwings and even 'the mounting Larks', who, as they prepare their song, 'fall, and leave their little Lives in Air' (109—34). Thunder is the term we found in the synecdoche describing English imperial conquest. There it operates to separate the real fact of artillery from the fantasy of the *pax Britannica*. Here it represents actual 'slaughter', but only in the dislocated pastoral world. The pheasant's bleeding — 'Short is his Joy! he feels the fiery Wound,/Flutters in Blood, and panting beats the Ground' (113—14) — brings the imagistic structure of the poem neatly full circle, to the imperial products that stand behind the colourful image of the pheasant: at the millennial climax of the poem these products, too, bleed and weep in sympathetic imitation — 'For me the Balm shall bleed, and Amber flow' (393).[43]

The birds are the suffering victims of imperial violence in the sylvan hunt, but they can only be recognized as victims so long as they remain birds. When this simile is reversed at the end of the poem, and the exploited peoples of British imperial expansion are likened to birds, we can see first of all how close birds and imperial victims are in the imagistic structure of the poem, but also how emphatically the evocation of suffering must then be denied:

Then Ships of uncouth Form shall stem the Tyde,
And Feather'd People crowd my wealthy Side,
And naked Youths and painted Chiefs admire
Our Speech, our Colour, and our strange Attire!
Oh stretch thy Reign, fair *Peace!* from Shore to Shore,
Till Conquest cease, and Slav'ry be no more:

Till the freed *Indians* in their native Groves
Reap their own Fruits, and woo their Sable Loves.
(403—10)

Here the people are feathered like birds. Their chiefs —
probably an allusion to the four Iroquois chiefs who
visited England in 1710[44] — are painted like the tragic
pheasant of the sylvan war. But in a shift symptomatic of
the ideology of the poem, these feathered creatures are not
victims; they are grateful beneficiaries and, like Pope,
celebrants of English imperialism. *Windsor-Forest* engages
in a process of exposing and concealing imperial power, a
dynamic like that which we observed in the relation
between the commodity and the epic in *The Rape of the
Lock*. In a sense, the poem's elaborate attempts to
rationalize imperial violence in the name of peace result in
a circular and obsessive return to the theme of violence
even in its most pastoral scenes. And this circularity is tied
to the poem's historical purpose. Politically, *Windsor-
Forest* celebrates the Peace of Utrecht, the coming of age
of English imperialism, and the fantasy of a millennial *pax
Britannica*, in which the 'sylvan Chace' will be the only
form of warfare, and liberty and concord will bring the
subject nations willingly to the 'wealthy side' of the
Thames. Utrecht was a Tory peace, negotiated over the
objections of the Whigs, who preferred an uncompromising
military victory. The Tories, billing themselves as compara-
tively peaceable, conceded territorial control in favour of
trading rights with the West Indies; it was as a result of this
Tory settlement, then, that England gained the slave
monopoly in the Spanish New World. This is the liberty
and concord that *Windsor* specifically defends and that
Pope offers both Whigs and Tories as a new aegis for class
and party unity. A few years later Pope confirmed his
allegiance to this ideal by investing £500 in the South Sea
Company, the beneficiary, though ultimately an unsuccess-
ful one, of Utrecht's mercantile gains.[45]

The plea of peace and liberty is one of the typical ideological reversals by which mercantile expansionism rationalizes itself in this period. In Pope's poetry, as we have seen, that claim involves a paradoxical conjunction of peace and violence. George Lillo's tragedy *The London Merchant* (1731) illustrates the same argument in simpler terms. The following representative encomium on trade occurs in a didactic dialogue between the merchant Thorowgood and his loyal apprentice Trueman:

> the method of merchandise ... is founded in reason and the nature of things ... it has promoted humanity, ... arts, industry, peace, and plenty; by mutual benefits diffusing mutual love from pole to pole. ... those countries where trade is promoted and encouraged do not make discoveries to destroy but to improve mankind — by love and friendship to tame the fierce and polish the most savage; to teach them the advantages of honest traffic by taking from them, with their own consent, their useless superfluities, and giving them in return what, from their ignorance in manual arts, their situation, or some other accident, they stand in need of. ... The populous East, luxuriant, abounds with glittering gems, bright pearls, aromatic spices, and health-restoring drugs. The late found western world glows with unnumbered veins of gold and silver ore. On every climate and on every country Heaven has bestowed some good peculiar to itself. It is the industrious merchant's business to collect the various blessings of each soil and climate and, with the product of the whole, to enrich his native country.[46]

Lillo's assertion is less elaborate than Pope's and therefore less formally fissured by the deep contradictions of imperialist ideology. In Pope's poem the catalogue of attractive commodities, the synecdoche, the uneasy oxymorons of the Eden scenes, the pastoral translation of imperial products, the reversal of vehicle and tenor, and the paradoxical displacement of violence — these interrelated formal structures together produce a vision of imperialism that unconsciously holds the attractions of accumulation in close proximity with the violence of exploitation. We can feel this tension most sharply in the pastoralization of imperial spoils: the flaming gold of mercantile accumulation is at the same time the colourful pheasant of the sylvan scene, and that bird is also the slaughtered victim of the *pax Britannica*. It may be no accident of aesthetic appreciation, then, that the pheasant passage is one of Pope's most famous. Maynard Mack writes that those lines 'remind us that Pope was an amateur painter and brought a subtler palette of color to English poetry than had appeared in it before', but that they are also 'less a description of "nature" in the Romantic sense than a moral *exemplum*, less about the beauty of pheasants than the transience of all beauty'.[47] This kind of tribute gives concrete force to Walter Benjamin's claim: 'There is no document of civilization which is not at the same time a document of barbarism.'[48] Mack sees only the 'document of civilization'. And indeed, taken independently, the effect of images like that of the pheasant is to conceal the violence of 'merchandise', the 'document of barbarism', and to produce the effect of universal aesthetic beauty that Mack appreciates. But taken as a whole, the process of displacement and inversion reveals the paradox of imperialist ideology with a special historical vision beyond Pope's and the poem's intentions.

III

In our readings of *The Rape of the Lock* and *Windsor-Forest* we have set up a constellation of interconnected formal and ideological structures, from rhetorical devices to generic and thematic conventions, and from concrete images of the products of trade to the subtle paradoxes of apology and propaganda. These structures have provided us with an introduction to the essential characteristics of

Pope's poetry, and to the essential contradictions of early imperialist ideology. We have surveyed the problem of Pope's — and perhaps also of any neo-classical writer's — use of Virgil and Homer. For Pope, classical allusion is simultaneously objective and subjective. As an external arbiter, it justifies his belief in imperialism and substantiates his critique of capitalism. As a construct of his own ideology, it precedes both justification and substantiation, taking its shape from the deepest contradictions of the age and giving those tensions their most eloquent expression. The dual position of neo-classicism in the ideological structure of Pope's poetry explains its local formal ambivalence, the indefinable shadings from irony to encomium, deflation to celebration, that mark its use. Virgil gives Pope the authority of an ancient tradition through which to validate his judgements of the present. But Virgil is also a product of Pope's present, shaped to fill the contradictory needs of a new imperialism. Thus he must serve as a nationalist and expansionist ideal, and yet sustain an anti-materialist moral standard: he must be the supreme exemplar of Augustan humanism.

The relationship of Pope's poetry to traditional genre is simply a more specific version of its ambiguous connection with the classics. The appeal in *The Rape of the Lock* to the classical epic and in *Windsor-Forest* to the pastoral georgic involves the same invocation of conventional authority, and again that authority turns out in the end to be the ideology of modern English imperialism. The objective and external literary structure becomes the subjective and self-generating aesthetic by which the paradoxes of the age are contained. But also exposed. Epic convention helps to moralize a materialist culture, or to launch a moral attack upon it, but the conjunction of epic and commodification reveals the contradiction in Pope's defence of empire. Pastoral serves to sublimate the violence and to naturalize the usurpation of mercantile imperialism, but the 'murdering guns' retain a prominent place in Pope's georgic, and the grotesque superimposition of mercantile spoils upon the English landscape demystifies the imperialist myth of self-determination for subject peoples.

In that myth, just as in Pope's classical allusions, subjective is projected as objective. As a neo-classicist, Pope writes his own Homer, and that text then serves as the arbiter of Pope's 'later' works. As an apologist for English imperialism, Pope constructs a referent — the image of a world of peace — which he can then claim as an external and prior justification for his belief. His poem thus works by reversing the terms by which history is understood: usurpation becomes self-determination, oppression liberty, and violence peace. The *pax Britannica* is a subjective rewriting of history represented as an objective account of reality. The dual status of the classics in Pope's works, then, could be said to replicate the structure of imperialist ideology itself, or, to reverse the terms, the ideology of imperialism could be said to echo the ambiguous position of neo-classicism in the literary culture of this period. Either way, the largest shapes of imperialist ideology and the most local forms of Pope's poems — including even stylistic details like oxymoron and synecdoche — are all parallel constituents of a single constellation of belief, discourse and apology.

We can take the central image of *The Rape of the Lock*, where Belinda regards her own figure in the mirror and creates herself, as a model for Pope's allusion to the classics and his dependence on conventional genre, as well as for his relation to any authoritative version of external 'Nature'. Belinda, like Pope's *Iliad* in his *Rape*, is ambiguously objective and subjective. She seems to be naturally beautiful, and yet her beauty must be made, and only in making it does she confirm its source in an external nature. She creates an extrinsic authority in her own image, just as Pope's allusion to Virgil or his use of classical genres provides a structure whose core is the ideology that his poetry expounds. Belinda's self-generating aesthetic derives from her tendency to merge with the commodity, and it produces a consequent problem of identity that we have already noted: which is Belinda and which is the goddess of the commodity? In the same way, *Windsor*'s ideology derives from the absorption of the products of trade into the English landscape. Which is the nation and which is the commodity? The poem's greatest insight is its failure to distinguish. Pope's greatest insight, too, may lie, ironically, in the inextricable dependence of his aesthetic upon the commodification of English culture. Which is the Augustan humanist and which the poet of the new age of the commodity? The mirror of 'True Wit' shows us both at once.

2   The 'New World' of
    Augustan Humanism:
    An Essay on Criticism (1711),
    An Essay on Man (1733–4)

We now turn to Pope's two major theoretical treatises, one aesthetic, the other philosophical. *An Essay on Criticism* was published in 1711, within two years of *Windsor-Forest* (1713) and the first version of *The Rape of the Lock* (1712). *An Essay on Man* was written between 1730 and 1734 and belongs to the last decade of Pope's poetic production. Our reading of Pope's theoretical works will thus require a chronological leap that parallels a division in Pope's poetic career between the early period of generic variety — the period represented by the first collected volume of Pope's *Works* in 1717 — and the late period of satire and philosophy. These two segments of the corpus of Pope's original poetry stand on either side of a decade of translations and editions — the *Iliad* (1715–20), the *Odyssey* (1725–6) and Shakespeare (1725). Readers of the whole of Pope's poetry have readily noticed an increasing bitterness in the satire, a growing anticipation of cultural collapse, and a related turn to grander, more systematic and more ambitious projects as that apocalypse apparently becomes more imminent.[1] Yet it is equally important to see the basic continuity in Pope's outlook throughout his career. Pope's works have their own history, but their historical importance, and their significance for this study, lie not so much in this private evolution as in their representation of the structures of thought of an age whose thinking is profoundly significant to the course of modern history.[2]

In fact throughout his career Pope remained committed to the project of forming a unified ruling class. As the son of a tradesman, Pope's associations with the aristocracy were inevitably those of an upwardly-mobile outsider, and this ambiguity in his class connections in part explains the double-edged attitude of admiration and contempt for the powerful landed families that we have already found in *The Rape of the Lock*. Nevertheless, Pope's social sympathies and friendships lay with the country aristocrats and prosperous landowners whom he viewed as the emblems of a progressive capitalist prosperity. And he considered this cultural ideal to be consistent with the mercantile interests responsible for the expansion of English overseas trade. In a sense Pope was ahead of his time. His early poetry, much of it written during the turbulent years surrounding the War of the Spanish Succession, coincides with a period of intense party strife within the upper classes and a frequent hostility between landed and business interests. The next fifty years, however, saw the gradual resolution of these conflicts and the formation of a narrow homogeneous ruling oligarchy sharing a broad community of interests and reinforced by pervasive family ties. This process of class consolidation, not yet completed at Pope's death, was none the less underway by the 1720s at the latest.[3] In general much of Pope's poetry seeks to persuade a class-divided audience that its interests could only be reconciled by means of aristocratic paternalism. Viewed from the perspective of the long-term creation of hegemony, *Windsor-Forest* in particular can be seen as a hortatory poem, an anticipatory attempt to fuse the still conflicting positions within the English upper classes into a unitary whole by offering the prospect of imperialist peace and prosperity.

It might seem surprising in this light that twenty years

later, when Pope's ruling-class vision was considerably closer to realization, he would find himself in opposition to the dominant government policy. Pope played a prominent role in the bi-partisan attack on Robert Walpole that progressively increased in strength during the decade of the 1730s. His second major period of poetic production roughly coincides with this political offensive. Significantly, Walpole's opponents accused him of reviving the 'invidious Distinction of the *landed* and *trading Interest*, which in Reality are always united; the *annual Rent* of Lands and the *Number of Years Purchase* having generally increased, or decreased, as *Trade* hath been more, or less flourishing.'[4] Further, although the Opposition highlighted the corruption of Walpole's ministry, the more decisive point, and the issue that eventually assured Walpole's fall from power, was his pacific foreign policy. Walpole would not go to war, except reluctantly and under great pressure in the last moments of his administration. He supported the large trading companies and the established commercial and financial interests, whose profits were steady and sure; but he had less sympathy for mercantile adventurers and for the more speculative schemes that fuelled an interest in an aggressively expansionist programme. Thus he repeatedly refused to extend, or even in some cases defend, England's commercial empire, despite the encroachments of other powers. The main political demand of the oppositional Patriots, the group for which Pope served as a kind of moral and cultural arbiter, was an aggressive struggle for an English share of Spain's South American and Pacific trade.[5]

The high moral claims of Pope's satires on the government and on contemporary society, then, are grounded in an imperialist content quite comparable to that of *Windsor-Forest*. In an ironic encomium to George II from the *Imitations of Horace*, *The First Epistle of the Second Book* (1737), Pope makes clear the source of his bitterness towards the current policy:

Oh! could I mount on the Mæonian wing,
Your Arms, your Actions, your Repose to sing!
What seas you travers'd! and what fields you fought!
Your Country's Peace, how oft, how dearly bought!
How barb'rous rage subsided at your word,
And Nations wonder'd while they dropp'd the sword!
How, when you nodded, o'er the land and deep,
Peace stole her wing, and wrapt the world in sleep.

(394—401)

The peaceful sleep of the conclusion of *The Dunciad* arises in part from this same imperialist position. Pope evokes Walpole, pilot of the ship of state, as Palinurus in the last lines of that poem:

Wide, and more wide, it spread o'er all the realm;
Ev'n Palinurus nodded at the Helm:
The Vapour mild o'er each Committee crept;
Unfinish'd Treaties in each Office slept;
And chiefless Armies doz'd out the Campaign;
And Navies yawn'd for Orders on the Main.

([B] IV, 613—18)

The *pax Britannica*, so firmly established in the rhetoric and ideological structures of *Windsor-Forest*, becomes a liability in the later works, as the relation between Pope's imperialist ideology and his perception of current foreign policy undergoes a diametrical reversal.

I

At first glance, the *Essay on Criticism* looks like a bad candidate for ideological critique. The poem has rarely been read in relation to the history of modern mercantile capitalist apology, and no wonder. Its announced subject — the nature of literary art and the correct mode of critical judgement — is so far from the explicit theme of *Windsor-Forest* that one might be tempted to think that

Pope's political concerns are restricted to that poem, and that the *Essay* treats a purely aesthetic topic. But ideology does not operate here and there, now determining the shape of discourse and now politely withdrawing from the scene to let the independent issues of true wit and critical judgement speak for themselves. We have already seen that there is no such independence, that those very issues are constituted by systems of thought and belief tied to the contradictions of contemporary history. In principle, there are no bad candidates for an ideological reading; the *Essay on Criticism* can enable us to explore that principle.

My point of entry is the poem's aesthetic terminology and forms of exemplification — the way it defines and illustrates wit, nature and the rules of art. This has been the main focus of critical discussions of the *Essay* since its first publication.[6] John Dennis, one of Pope's contemporaries, took issue with the use of 'Nature' in the poem,[7] and since then reader after reader has displayed, attacked, sought to reconcile or undertaken to explain Pope's ambiguous terminology. Literary historians have seen Pope's verbal tricks as evidence of a major terminological shift between the aesthetic usages of the seventeenth and those of the nineteenth centuries.[8] Modern defenders of Pope's ambiguity have described his aesthetic as uniquely generous, encompassing and flexible in its interpretation of neo-classical doctrine, uniquely humane in its inclusion of divergent redactions of classical authority.[9] We will instead attempt to enlist the difficulty of the poem's terminology on the side of demystification, to see in the problem of aesthetic categories a particular ideological configuration whose complexities account for the poem's verbal ambiguities. In speaking of wit and nature, the *Essay on Criticism* provides one peculiarly problematic version of the ideology of mercantile capitalism. It joins the representation of the structural principles of a capitalist social order with an informing image of imperial expansion. We must explore both the principles and the problems of its system.

The debate over the *Essay*'s terminology can be briefly canvassed. It centres on the words 'wit' and 'nature', each of which has a variety of meanings and valences.[10] Wit ranges in definition from frivolous verbal ingenuity to true creative invention. It is associated both with judgement and with a potentially irrational separate force.[11] And its exploitation can be either 'glorious' (152) — the indication of true greatness — or dangerous:

> For *Works* may have more *Wit* than does 'em good,
> As *Bodies* perish through Excess of Blood.
>
> (303—4)

The dangers raised by wit are significantly resonant. They resemble Dulness's later apocalyptic verbal excesses in *The Dunciad*: 'One *glaring Chaos* and *wild Heap* of *Wit*' (292). And they are connected with social disorder and the blasphemous attack on traditional religion that Pope associates with the vicious and lewd writers of the Restoration when '*Wits* had *Pensions*, and *young Lords* had *Wit*' (539). Wit, then, is both trivially extrinsic and generatively immanent, and the valence of its operations fundamentally ambiguous. So too with nature. In phrases like 'the Face of Nature' (313) and 'the *naked Nature* and the *living Grace*' (294), nature is an external aesthetic object to be accurately represented by the true artist, not falsely obscured with 'gawdy Colours' (312), '*Gold* and *Jewels*', or other '*Ornaments*' (295—6). But nature can also be the ordering principle of the universe, the Deity, or the first cause:

> *Unerring Nature*, still divinely bright,
> One *clear, unchang'd*, and *Universal* Light,
> Life, Force, and Beauty, must to all impart.
>
> (70—2)

This notion comes to Pope from Renaissance neo-Platonic thought, as does the parallel sense of nature as the '*glimm'ring Light*' (21) of human reason, the evidence of the imitation of God's universal reason in the mind of man. Nature thus serves for the poem both as the object of mimesis and as the ordering principle — the process of perception by which that reality is understood. On the one hand, then, the *Essay* claims to describe the reproduction of an external reality and the ways in which that reproduction should be evaluated But at the same time the poem produces that reality by locating it in the subjective processes of artistic creation. This is Pope's version of an old philosophical paradox, for which we must find an ideological location.

Indeed we have already begun to do so with our discussion of the problem of 'True Wit' in *The Rape of the Lock*. That touchstone couplet, and its succeeding elaboration, summarizes the paradox of the *Essay on Criticism*:

> *True Wit* is *Nature* to Advantage drest,
> What oft was *Thought*, but ne'er so well *Exprest*,
> *Something*, whose Truth convinc'd at Sight we find,
> That gives us back the Image of our Mind.
>
> (297–300)

The second couplet draws on the notion that, since man is created in God's image, the operations of human reason or wit in creating a work of art imitate the divine reason that creates and orders nature. Hence to represent nature might mean either to represent God's creation or to represent ourselves, our own systems of order and knowledge. The image here is very close to that of the mirror in the toilet scene of *The Rape of the Lock*. Just as Belinda observes herself in the glass and creates herself as an external and objective other, Pope in the *Essay on Criticism* sees the shape of his own thought as objective nature. But in this poem that process is formulated not in terms of the commodities of a young lady's dressing table, but in terms of the tenets of neo-classical aesthetics: the preoccupation with eternal truths and universal human experience contained in the concept of general nature; the conjunction of a cosmic order and the ordering faculty of wit; the commitment to regularity, harmony and the reconciliation of opposition or contradiction; and the claim to an absolute structuring principle implicit in nature itself and translatable through all levels and kinds of discourse. How does mercantile capitalism enter here?

We have already seen in Denham's *Cooper's Hill* that the distinctive balanced effects of the heroic couplet can be linked to thematic concerns with balanced government and an ordered mercantile exchange. Such a direct reciprocity is not available in the *Essay on Criticism*, but an equally reciprocal, if less direct, connection will emerge from a close examination of the poem's representations of balance and order. The *Essay*'s typical couplet form is among the most closed and antithetical in Pope's works. Its verse imitates the totalizing, hierarchical system of nature that it describes, and that system is in turn substantiated by the ordered aesthetic universe of the poem. The symmetry of the system is evident in the *Essay*'s opening paragraph — '*Writing*' and '*Judging*', '*Patience*' and '*Sense*', 'few' and 'Numbers', '*that*' and '*this*':

> 'Tis hard to say, if greater Want of Skill
> Appear in *Writing* or in *Judging* ill;
> But, of the two, less dang'rous is th' Offence,
> To tire our *Patience*, than mis-lead our *Sense*:
> Some few in *that*, but Numbers err in *this*,
> Ten Censure wrong for one who Writes amiss.
>
> (1—6)

A recent critic of the couplet form has argued that the 'logical and structural closure' of the verse, with its aphoristic quality, 'becomes a way of seeing things whole'. This kind of poetry is preceptual rather than progressive, it records a proposition rather than a movement, and hence it 'suggests a view of subject or reality as existing rather than developing, as a field rather than a process'.[12] Especially in the opening lines of the *Essay on Criticism*, Pope's verse is based upon the schematic arrangement not of verbs but of static noun forms:

> In *Poets* as true *Genius* is but rare,
> True *Taste* as seldom is the *Critick*'s Share.
>
> (11—12)

> *Authors* are partial to their *Wit*, 'tis true,
> But are not *Criticks* to their *Judgment* too?
>
> (17–18)

> Each burns alike, who can, or cannot write,
> Or with a *Rival*'s, or an *Eunuch*'s spite.
>
> (30–1)

> Launch not beyond your Depth, but be discreet,
> And mark *that Point* where Sense and Dulness *meet*.
>
> (50–1)

As these examples suggest, the beginning of the poem — like similar passages in the *Essay on Man* — sets up a static, ordered universe dependent on a set of poetic congruities. It proposes a mode of discourse in which every concept has its place in relation to every other, where contrasting nouns are linked to form a syntactic whole and contrarities are made to co-operate in a kind of grammatical counterpart of *concordia discors*. In a discussion of the nature of Pope's rhymes, Hugh Kenner has provided a perspective that might stand as a conditional general assessment of the ideology of Pope's poetic practice. Kenner suggests that Pope's couplet is structured to hint at a fantasy of propriety, wholeness and universal truth, that Pope's poetry figures the conviction 'that the world bespeaks order and congruence', and that the 'details of language should mirror this congruence'.[13] We might add that the denial of conflict and difference is one of the operative tenets of this conviction, and that the resultant totalizing prosody works to stave off contradiction, to construct a hierarchy of meaning and value, and to validate a stratified stasis. This prosody, we could say, evinces a powerful will to order. We shall see this order countered, subverted and overrun in Pope's poetry, especially in the catalogue rhetoric of *The Dunciad*. But not in the *Essay on Criticism*. Here theme neatly conforms to prosody at every turn.

The poem opens by proposing that '*Writing*' (or poetry) and '*Judging*' (or criticism) are parallel but contrasting, complementary acts, each with a complete set of similarly parallel attributes: genius and taste, wit and judgment, colouring and learning. The *Essay* extends this aesthetic system next to the order of the external world:

> As on the *Land* while *here* the *Ocean* gains,
> In *other Parts* it leaves wide sandy Plains.
>
> (54—5)

And the system goes on to determine the inner logic of the human soul, where '*Understanding*' gives way to '*Memory*', and '*Memory*' to '*Imagination*' (56—9) in a neat and comprehensive hierarchy. The order represented here is complete and closed. Because the contrasting nouns seem to name antithetical poles, their juxtaposition — poetry and criticism, land and ocean, understanding and imagination — appears to include all that might lie between. Though few qualities are named, it seems that nothing is left out.

That impression is confirmed in the early passages on nature. Nature is unerring, unchanged and universal, the imparter of life, force and beauty, and the source and end of art (68—73). It fixes the limits of human capacity, defining the proper place of human endeavour in the vast system that it comprehends (50—67). These limits, then, are not external controls asserted against nature, but internal boundaries included in the very definition of nature as universal order. The perspective that Pope expounds here combines what we have already designated as the neo-Platonic belief in an ordering principle that determines the logic of the universe, with the Renaissance notion of a chain of being where everything has its proper place in a hierarchy that stretches from inanimate matter to God and includes all creation.[14] We will find this latter idea more fully elaborated in the *Essay on Man*. The *Essay on Criticism* builds its aesthetic system out of these traditional cosmologies, constructing a definition of art simultaneously with its description of nature. 'True Wit' reproduces nature, embodies its ordering powers and gives expression to its coherence. Aesthetic rules, like the fit limits of nature, are not externally imposed, but already present, to be discovered and codified by those first great poets, the ancients. Thus nature and art merge in the language of the poem, each serving reciprocally to illuminate the other. The first long encomium to nature shows how intimate the two categories become:

> First follow NATURE, and your Judgment frame
> By her just Standard, which is still the same;
> *Unerring Nature* . . .
> Life, Force, and Beauty, must to all impart,
> At once the *Source*, and *End*, and *Test* of *Art*.
> *Art* from that Fund each *just Supply* provides,
> Works *without Show*, and *without Pomp* presides.
>
> (68—75)

Nature, art's source, is also reproduced in art, as art's sole end. Each operates by the same rules, and each serves as a metaphor for the other: nature imparts beauty to the world like an artist, and the artist participates in the generative powers of nature. The aesthetic system of the poem is thus explained and justified by its identity with a closed, totalizing cosmic system, and that system, too, is rationalized by its imitation of the system of aesthetics. But what is this metaphysical order upon which Pope constructs his aesthetic theory? Is it simply a philosophical abstraction with an intellectual history in neo-Platonism and Renaissance cosmology? It certainly comes in part from the past, but what is its use in the present?

The immanence of classical rules in the order of art, as we have already seen, reflects the inherent limits in the cosmic system of nature. Both, however, are defined in relation to a social system, a system based on natural law:

> Those RULES of old *discover'd*, not *devis'd*,
> Are *Nature* still, but *Nature Methodiz'd*;
> *Nature*, like *Liberty*, is but restrain'd
> By the same Laws which first *herself* ordain'd.
>
> (88—91)

The passage moves from art to nature to society, in the form of law and liberty. Indeed, the juxtaposition between liberty and law seems to be the ground of the contrast between nature and nature's limits: art and nature provide secondary versions of a primary social order. The appearance of the law here is no accident. Once again, Pope echoes a set of established conventions, but this time they are conventions of capitalist social theory. The power of the law and its connection with liberty is one of the central tenets of eighteenth-century bourgeois thought. Law imposes a uniform constraint upon social actions, a constraint based not on social status but on the nature of the action itself. It represents the establishment of the notion of individual civic responsibility and, relatedly, of individual rights, since the state is created by mutual consent to guarantee liberty through law. Thus law prevents tyranny while it creates the possibility of a civil authority.

One of the main sources for this doctrine of reverence for the law is John Locke, whose summary of the issues indicates the complex centrality of the idea:

> But though [the state of nature] be a state of liberty, yet it is not a state of licence; though man in that state have an uncontrollable liberty to dispose of his person or possessions, yet he has not liberty to destroy himself, or so much as any creature in his possession, but where some nobler use than its bare preservation calls for it. The state of nature has a law of nature to govern it which obliges every one; and reason, which is that law, teaches all mankind who will but consult it that, being all equal and independent, no one ought to harm another in his life, health, liberty, or possessions.[15]

Defoe, in an entry in the *Review* (1711), supplies a less abstract, more polemical version of the conjunction of liberty and law and its significance in the political thought of the period:

> In *England*, even the Soveraign never punishes but by
> Law, and a Jury of Equals must determine the Fact
> .... Obedience to the Law is all the Subjection,
> *speaking of Human Affairs*, that either GOD or the
> QUEEN requires. ...
>
> 'Tis a happy thing, Gentlemen, to live under the
> Laws of *ENGLAND* ... an *English* Man is born a
> Free Man, no Power can insult him, no Superior
> oppress him; The Law only is his Governour; no
> Magistrate, no Counsellor, no Authority, no not the
> Soveraign has the least illegal Power over him; he can
> have no Sentence pronounced against him, no Punish-
> ment inflicted, no Fine levied, no not by the QUEEN
> Her self, but according to Law. ...
>
> He that will abandon this Liberty, is not a Fool
> only, but a Knave.[16]

This incipient political theme brings with it a reading of
English history. Pope alludes in the *Essay* to the thesis of
what we might call early bourgeois historiography: that
liberty belongs to the pre-Norman or 'Gothic' period when
the primitive Anglo-Saxons or 'Britons' were thought to
have introduced parliamentary government. In this view,
the tradition of Magna Carta, on which the revolution of
1688 founded itself, was simply a return to pre-Norman
laws.[17] When Pope refers to the 'brave *Britons*' (715),
then, he is referring to this heritage of parliamentary
power, just as when he describes poets as heirs of a
primitive, ancient tradition:

> Poets, a *Race* still unconfin'd and free,
> Still fond and proud of *Savage Liberty*.
>
> (649–50)

This historical view of English liberty has a destination in
the present, in the panegyric to prosperity, commerce and
empire that we have already found to be so prominent in
the period. In one contemporary work, ' 'Tis *Property*
supports *Pursuit*:/*Freedom* gives Eloquence; and *Freedom*,

gain.'[18] Pope's poem equates the natural law through which liberty must be preserved with just government and imperial expansion, seen as the exportation of art:

> Thus long succeeding Criticks justly reign'd,
> *Licence* repress'd, and *useful Laws* ordain'd;
> *Learning* and *Rome* alike in Empire grew,
> And *Arts* still *follow'd* where her *Eagles flew*.
>
> (681—4)

Alternatively, Charles II's promiscuous court — illustrative of an era of false wit — provides a negative example of the connection of true wit and imperialism:

> When *Love* was all an easie Monarch's Care;
> Seldom at *Council*, never in a *War*:
> *Jilts* rul'd the State, and Statesmen *Farces* writ;
> Nay *Wits* had *Pensions*, and *young Lords* had *Wit*.
>
> (536—9)

A failure in imperialist foreign policy is automatically equated with aesthetic failure. In the early editions of the poem William III comes in for a similar attack symptomatic of the poem's covert politics: William was guilty of a failure to maintain a favourable balance of trade with the Dutch, traditional imperial rivals of England in the seventeenth century, who in this couplet illegitimately enjoy English gold in exchange only for the influence of what Pope considered a bankrupt morality:

> Then *first* the *Belgian Morals* were extoll'd;
> We their *Religion* had, and they our *Gold*.[19]

These metaphors illustrate the inextricable intertwining of politics and aesthetics in the *Essay*. In their interdependence we can see circulating the main ideological categories of the poem: art, liberty, order, justice, fundamental or natural law, cultural nationalism and imperial expansion.

Indeed that last, seemingly supplementary matter of imperialism is actually a constitutive category both of the

Essay's ideology and of its aesthetic: this poem, like *Windsor-Forest* and *The Rape of the Lock*, is informed by the multivalent image of the New World. In *Windsor-Forest* we documented a reciprocal structure in which England's pastoral landscape becomes indistinguishable from the commodities of mercantile expansion: 'the new World launch[es] forth to seek the Old' (402) and the old world stretches its reign across the new, to the 'freed *Indians*', Peru, and the 'other *Mexico's*' of the *pax Britannica* (409–12). We have already seen how Pope connects the arts with imperial expansion in the *Essay on Criticism*. Such a conjunction is a strong motif in the period. Edward Young, like many other writers, sees the link as part of the happy destiny and responsibility of the *pax Britannica*:

> COMMERCE gives Arts, as well as *Gain*;
> By Commerce wafted o'er the Main
> *They* barbarous Climes enlighten as they run;
> *Arts* the rich Traffic of the Soul!
> May travel *thus*, from Pole to Pole,
> And gild the World with Learning's *brighter* Sun.
>
> *Commerce* gives *Learning, Virtue, Gold!*
> Ply *Commerce*, then, ye *Britons* bold.[20]

The *Essay on Criticism* makes the connection by way of the classical writers, the true and originary representatives of both art and nature. The classics call up the image of Roman imperialism, and that image is projected from the '*happier Days*' of the past into the new worlds of a future imperial exploration:

> Hail *Bards Triumphant*! born in *happier Days*;
> *Immortal* Heirs of *Universal* Praise!
> . . .
> Nations *unborn* your mighty Names shall sound,
> And Worlds applaud that must not yet be *found*!
>
> (189–94)

But the *Essay*'s new worlds are also found in art itself.

When the poet, in his transient moment of power, puts pen to paper:

> . . . a *new World* leaps out at his command,
> And ready Nature waits upon his Hand.
>
> (486–7)

Art creates the same new worlds that expansionist culture discovers and exploits. The 'other *Mexico's*' of Pope's poetry, then, are both distant places — different, external and exotic — and internal, domestic landscapes, inherent in the autonomous power of the individual creative genius. Pope's aesthetic argument at this point reproduces the ideological structure of his most explicit apology for imperialism — *Windsor-Forest*. Both poems subscribe to the same fantasy of reciprocal power and appropriation, the same image of a simultaneously internal and external new world, though the *Essay* translates that fantasy from imperial to aesthetic terms. As we have seen, the *Essay*'s account of art is based in the notions of social order, just government and imperial expansion that ground the mercantile capitalist state. The new world of art, then, has the same crucial place in Pope's aesthetic as the actual New World in the expansionist ideology of the age.

The equation of the new world of the artist with that of the imperialist represents an innovative conjunction of a pair of traditions that Pope inherits from the Renaissance. The view of the artist as a version of the deity, making new worlds in the same way that God created this one, is typical of Renaissance neo-Platonic thought. Its most influential English expression occurs in Sidney's *Apologie for Poetrie* (1595):

> Onely the Poet, disdayning to be tied to any such subiection, lifted vp with the vigor of his owne inuention, dooth growe in effect another nature, in making things either better then Nature bringeth forth, or, quite a newe, formes such as neuer were in

Nature, . . . Nature neuer set forth the earth in so rich
tapistry as diuers Poets haue done, neither with
plesant riuers, fruitful trees, sweet smelling flowers,
nor whatsoeuer els may make the too much loued
earth more louely. Her world is brasen, the Poets
only deliuer a golden.[21]

The other Renaissance 'new world' tradition arises directly
from the voyages of discovery and includes both exotic
descriptions of a geographical New World and imaginary
renditions of Utopian or anti-Utopian other worlds made
possible by the widening of physical perspective in the
sixteenth century. These travel narratives, both 'real' and
'imaginary', are equally adventurous. Sixteenth- and
seventeenth-century accounts of Virginia, New England
and the West Indies, though often designed primarily to
encourage commerce and colonization, deliberately dwell
upon the strange and the picturesque. The sustained
popularity of the famous encyclopaedic travel narratives
of the period, Richard Hakluyt's *Principall Navigations*
(1589) and Samuel Purchas's *Purchas his Pilgrimes* (1625),
indicates both the prominence and the mixed role — geographical, patriotic, religious and imaginative — of exploration and discovery.[22]

In the preface to his first volume, Purchas gives us a hint
of the convergence of these 'vncouth Countries' and
Sidney's 'other nature':

My *Genius* delights rather in by-wayes then high-
wayes, and hath therein by Tracts and Tractates of
Trauellers made Causies and High-wayes, euery where
disposing these Pilgrime-Guides, that men without
feare may trauell to and ouer the most vncouth
Countries of the World: and there be shewed with
others Eyes, the Rarities of Nature, and of such things
also as are not against Nature, but either aboue it, as
Miracles, or beside the ordinarie course of it, in the extraordinary Wonders, which Gods Prouidence hath therein
effected according to his good and iust pleasure.[23]

The reader of Purchas's book is a traveller to other worlds, just as the reader of the 'imaginary' voyage of discovery in Thomas More's *Utopia* encounters a new world that is empowered by the actual voyages of discovery but that generates a separate image, new but also familiar, 'formes such as neuer were in Nature' and yet 'not against Nature'. The social force of *Utopia* rests on precisely this conjunction of the familiar and the strange, or rather the familiar made strange and the strange made familiar in contemporary society. More's work, like Pope's, brings the exotic home, superimposing the indigenous upon the foreign, the New World upon the green and pleasant landscape of England, in a reciprocal move that constitutes its meaning.

Pope's natural and even automatic equation of these two Renaissance new world motifs makes their historical connection even more apparent. They arise together, they share a common language and terminology, and together they express the opening up of European culture to the humanist and individualist strains of early bourgeois thought. The autonomous artist, like the proto-imperialist, leaps over the boundaries of the old world in order to empower himself as the deity of a new one, just as Prospero in *The Tempest* directs the fates of the visitors to his island, and Captain James Cook encouraged the awe-struck Hawaiians to believe that he was the white god Lono, returned from across the seas. Prospero repudiates his magic. Cook was struck down when his worshippers saw that he could bleed. In Pope's poetry such a direct reversal is impossible, but a faint qualification of this appropriation of power can be seen in the contingency and transience of Pope's account of artistic production, when *'failing Language'* cuts short the life of *'Modern Rhymes'*, and when, just as the poet's new world attains 'full Perfection', 'all the bright Creation fades away!' (476—93).

We can find another version of this qualification in the evasiveness of the *Essay*'s aesthetic theory, an evasiveness directly tied to a symptomatic political inconsistency. Despite the poem's grounding in Lockean notions of social

order and just government, the *Essay*'s treatment of these
bourgeois ideals is sometimes incongruously ambiguous.
For example, in its justification of neo-classical rules, as
we have seen, the poem presents those rules in terms of
bourgeois law, inherent in the concept of liberty and
therefore built into the system of order by which the
whole structure of society and art must stand. But the
famous passage on the sublime permits an occasional
disobedience of the rules, entirely inconsistent with that
structure:

> Great Wits sometimes may *gloriously offend*,
> And *rise* to *Faults* true Criticks *dare not mend*;
> From *vulgar Bounds* with *brave Disorder* part,
> And *snatch* a *Grace* beyond the Reach of Art,
> . . .
> But tho' the *Ancients* thus their *Rules* invade,
> (As *Kings* dispense with *Laws* Themselves have made)
> *Moderns*, beware!
>
> (152—63)

Significantly, Pope labels this illegality 'Licence' (149),
a term often used in the period to evoke aristocratic
privilege or absolutist tyranny in contrast to bourgeois
law. The OED cites from 1720 the pat opposition 'They
are for licence, not for liberty', and Pope himself
contrasts the two in describing the ancient critics who
'justly reign'd,/*Licence* repress'd, and *useful Laws*
ordain'd' (681—2). In bourgeois society by definition
no one is above the law, and no distinction between the
rights of the governing and those of the 'vulgar' is
possible. This passage seems to suggest instead the
prerogative of the monarch in an absolutist state, where
the notion of royal licence signifies the unrestricted
powers of the king. Under absolutism, though there is
order, there are no laws by which all are equally bound.
The turn to an absolutist political metaphor is especially
interesting here because the eighteenth-century sublime,
in its disregard for rules, tended to be associated with

bourgeois notions of creative autonomy and individualism, and even with the rough, the wild and the
'vulgar'. Pope locates the most progressive or transitional
point of his aesthetics in the most reactionary political
theory available to him. This double historical
perspective is symptomatic of the ideology of Pope's
poetic form. We shall see the same strange conjunction
of progressive and reactionary impulses in *The Dunciad*.

The matter is complicated further by the historical
passage that concludes the *Essay*:

> But *we*, brave *Britons, Foreign Laws* despis'd,
> And kept *unconquer'd*, and *unciviliz'd*,
> Fierce for the *Liberties of Wit*, and bold,
> We still defy'd the *Romans*, as *of old*.
> Yet *some* there were, among the *Sounder Few*
> Of those who *less presum'd*, and *better knew*,
> Who durst assert the *juster Ancient Cause*,
> And here *restor'd* Wit's *Fundamental Laws*.
>
> (715–22)

These lines make a number of familiar allusions: to
'*Fundamental Laws*', the '*Liberties of Wit*' and the '*un-
conquer'd*' Britons of the 'Gothic' period. But they make
other more problematic connections as well. 'Restoration'
is at this time generally equated with the restoration of
the monarchy in 1660, the period of Roscomon, as the
passage goes on to specify. Pope clearly means to evoke
this typical positive association of restoration with the re-
establishment of social order, but we have already seen
that he is not favourably disposed towards Charles II — his
was an age of licence, not a reign of true wit, just government or a sufficiently aggressive imperialism. By the same
token, the association of the rules with France in the immediately preceding lines (711–14) contributes to the
impression — when 'Wit's *Fundamental Laws*' are restored
under Charles II — that those laws have some connection
with the absolutist political aspirations that Charles shared
with Louis XIV. In other words, the metaphor for

bourgeois law briefly overlaps with one for absolute monarchy. Indeed, if we look too closely, the political material that we have found to be so pervasive in the poem seems to fragment or to turn upon itself. The problem here is neatly summarized in an earlier variant of the central passage on aesthetic rules at the beginning of the *Essay*:

> Those RULES of old *discover'd*, not *devis'd*,
> Are *Nature* still, but *Nature Methodiz'd*;
> *Nature*, like *Liberty*, is but restrain'd
> By the same Laws which first *herself* ordain'd.
>
> (88—91)

Through all the early editions of the *Essay*, up until Pope's final revision in 1743, the second couplet read not '*Liberty*' but:

> *Nature*, like *Monarchy*, is but restrain'd
> By the same Laws which first *herself* ordain'd.[24]

The laws that monarchy ordains are very different from those of liberty. This substitution in the basic metaphor for aesthetic order signals a crucial confusion in the political imagery that governs the ideological structure of the poem — a confusion between the bourgeois state and a moderate absolutism. Perhaps this political incoherence can serve as a sign of Pope's own reservations about bourgeois hegemony, despite his acceptance of the general contours of contemporary social thought. More broadly, however, this ambivalence reproduces the compromise of post-revolutionary English society, in which the monarchy anomalously survived the bourgeois revolution and lived on, with some of its power and much of its cultural significance intact, at least into the nineteenth century.

We can now return, with more ideological ammunition, to the problems of terminology with which we began. Pope's ambiguous use of 'nature' and 'wit' is linked directly to the ideological confusion that we have discovered in the poem. The sliding definition of nature — from object of mimesis to ordering principle and from cosmic system to divine creative power — enables the poem to move from regulated civic responsibility to divinely authorized licence and back again, in other words to shift the ideological systems of order upon which its notions of art and society are founded. When Pope's vexed affirmation of bourgeois law gives way to absolutist licence, his aesthetic terminology can follow suit. The various definitions of wit similarly derive their range from Pope's ambivalence about bourgeois liberty. True wit may be the possession either of the law-abiding citizen or the licentious king. To snatch at wit by transgressing the laws of art may indicate genius, pride or folly, since it may represent a dangerous violation of the terms of civic order or a built-in and appropriate act of power in a hierarchical system. Wherever the *Essay* moves in relation to law, order and autonomy, wit moves too. We might even say that the fact that these various definitions of wit are available to Pope at this moment in the history of aesthetic theory makes it possible for the *Essay* to express the complications and contradictions of his ideology. Or that the terminological confusions of the *Essay* and the period are partly the consequences of a particular post-revolutionary, early capitalist ideological configuration, in which crucial problems with the nature of order and the locus of power have a prominent place. The ambiguities of the terms wit and nature, then, constitute an available vocabulary of contradiction, a language in which the tensions of the age can be written.

That is the language I have tried to read in *An Essay on Criticism*. The poem renders its aesthetic theory in terms of the ideological contradiction that we have found thus far to be typical of Pope's major works. It sees art through the lens of the mercantile capitalist state, constructing an aesthetics out of the logic of bourgeois social order. But, like the ironic mock-heroic duality in *The Rape of the Lock* or the anti-imperialist images of violence in *Windsor-Forest*, the poem undercuts its own system, unconsciously questioning the new mode of production upon which it builds itself. For this reason it is hard to tell — or perhaps simply irrelevant to ask — where Pope stands. He seems to stand both inside and outside bourgeois culture, celebrating and satirizing the goddess of the commodity, building an aesthetics of bourgeois hegemony with the artefacts of absolutism.

II

In the *Essay on Criticism* we located a vocabulary of contradiction, a fluid poetic language that enables Pope's discourse to operate at a variety of levels — cosmic, aesthetic and political — and to carry without collision a variety of contradictory meanings — individualist, bourgeois and absolutist. *An Essay on Man* makes a parallel use of imagery. Though its basic terminology is relatively stable, at least compared to the elusiveness of wit and nature in the *Essay on Criticism*, its central images introduce a formal instability parallel to that of the earlier work and indicative of a complex of contradictions that place the poem's philosophical premises in question. The problem begins with Pope's allusions to himself. In *The Rape of the Lock* he quotes himself as Homer, and the mock-heroic ironies of that poem derive in part from his ventriloquization of an external authority. In the *Essay on Man* he quotes himself directly, taking his own early work as his text. The intermediary here is not Homer but Pope's period of classical translation and edition, the gap in his poetic career between the first collected *Works* and the late poems. Indeed we shall find, especially in our study of *The Dunciad*, that the major poems at the end of Pope's career consistently recall phrases, images, themes and passing moments from his earlier works. In the *Essay on Man*, and also in *The Dunciad*, the relationship between the earlier and the later poems is unclear, strained and inverted. Pope rarely quotes himself with simple approval, and he rarely places this kind of self-reference in the same context as the original. The result is a tension that signals the central ideological problems of Pope's poetry.

Near the beginning of the *Essay*'s first epistle, following the opening description of the chain of being and the 'general Order *of things*' within which man must accept his proper 'place *and* rank', Pope supplies an illustration of his assertion that human happiness depends upon man's 'ignorance *of* future *events, and* ... hope *of a* future *state*' ('Argument of the First Epistle'):

> Lo! the poor Indian, whose untutor'd mind
> Sees God in clouds, or hears him in the wind;
> His soul proud Science never taught to stray
> Far as the solar walk, or milky way;
> Yet simple Nature to his hope has giv'n,
> Behind the cloud-topt hill, an humbler heav'n;
> Some safer world in depth of woods embrac'd,
> Some happier island in the watry waste,
> Where slaves once more their native land behold,
> No fiends torment, no Christians thirst for gold!
>
> (I, 99—108)

The immediate relevance of this image is obvious. It derives in part from the Deist concern — well established by the eighteenth century — that pagans ignorant of revelation must not by that accident be excluded from God's mercy. Pope may have recalled Dryden's passage on the 'Indian Souls' in *Religio Laici* (1682):

> 'Tis said the sound of a *Messiah's Birth*
> Is gone through all the habitable Earth:
> But still that Text must be confin'd alone
> To what was *then* inhabited, and known:
> And what Provision cou'd from *thence* accrue
> To *Indian* Souls, and Worlds discover'd *New*?[25]

But Pope's 'poor Indian' dreaming of slaves who once more behold their native land has a different resonance from Dryden's '*Indian* Souls'. Slavery, as we have discovered, is a central conscious and unconscious feature of

Windsor-Forest, and that poem provides a detailed prior model for the *Essay*'s image of pagan hope:

> Oh stretch thy Reign, fair *Peace!* from Shore to Shore,
> Till Conquest cease, and Slav'ry be no more:
> Till the freed *Indians* in their native Groves
> Reap their own Fruits, and woo their Sable Loves,
> *Peru* once more a Race of Kings behold,
> And other *Mexico's* be roof'd with Gold.
>
> (407—12)

The conjunction of slavery, native lands, gold and the Indians who are made to behold and bear witness to their own future for the edification and consolation of an English audience links these passages directly with one another. The 'freed Indians' in *Windsor-Forest* embody the imperialist fantasy of power without violence, exploitation without slavery. The 'poor Indian' of the *Essay on Man* also enacts a fantasy of power, but one located in the present rather than the future — a fantasy of the quiescence and collaboration of the oppressed. The Indian will submit to slavery, torment and expropriation without resistance because 'Hope springs eternal in the human breast' (I, 95): he has his own pathetic belief in a world without slavery, as impossible as that of *Windsor-Forest*. This belief, which includes his hope that 'His faithful dog shall bear him company' (I, 112) in that happier land, is explicitly ridiculed in Epistle IV, where Pope attacks the fools who form concrete expectations about the rewards of heaven:

> Go, like the Indian, in another life
> Expect thy dog, thy bottle, and thy wife.
>
> (IV, 177—8)

We know the Indian's expectations are false, and yet he is meant to serve as an example to the poem's audience, to teach us to 'Submit — In this, or any other sphere,/Secure to be as blest as thou canst bear' (I, 285—6). The crux of the problem in this passage is the representation of power. The parallel with *Windsor-Forest* emphasizes the connection of the image of the Indian with the violence of imperialism. Though Pope's reference to 'fiends', 'Christians' and 'gold' in the *Essay* directs his attack at the Spanish, we know his own and England's complicity in the West Indian slave trade. English traders, of course, dealt primarily in African rather than Native American slaves, and English settlers in the New World had a less explicitly genocidal programme than the Spanish. But the Native Americans who came in contact with English imperialism would be as likely as those who met the Spanish to wish for a 'safer world'. In the century before the writing of *Windsor-Forest*, English settlers in North America had fought a virtually continuous war with the coastal tribes: the most notable conflicts being the Pequot War (1636–7), the Wampanoag King Philip's War (1675–6), the Tuscarora War (1711–13), and the Yamasee War (1715). By the first quarter of the eighteenth century these tribes were essentially destroyed, their populations reduced to a fraction by battle, massacre, disease or sale into slavery. During the campaign against the Pequot nation of the Connecticut River Valley, a large segment of the tribe was slain at a single famous massacre in which a fortified village was burned to the ground and the fleeing populace picked off by colonial and 'friendly' native troops stationed around the circumference; this victory was succeeded by a genocidal hunt for the remnants of the tribe. King Philip's War, a much lengthier and broader conflict, involved a loose confederation of tribes, nominally headed by Philip, a Wampanoag leader renamed by the colonists. The battles, sieges and raids of this war ranged across Massachusetts, Rhode Island, Connecticut and what is now New Hampshire, while the Tuscarora and Yamasee Wars were restricted to the Carolinas. Throughout this period it was common practice to sell the captured natives into slavery either in the Virginia colonies or the West Indies, and by this means, as well as through the depradations of the Carolinian slave raiders upon the mission Indians of Florida, significant numbers of the coastal Native Americans became slaves.

The Peace of Utrecht, in the context of the concession of the Hudson Bay Territory to England, pronounced the peoples of the great Iroquois Confederacy of the Mohawk River Valley British subjects. The Iroquois themselves had no voice in this decree. In the succeeding years before the official outbreak of war with France in 1756, English colonists made a series of desultory efforts to enlist these new 'subjects' against the French settlers. During the first stage of the French and Indian War, Native American warriors did some of the fighting as proxies for the two European imperialist powers, and the forced and arbitrary division of the Indian nations among the French and English sometimes pitted members of the same tribe against one another.

Even when armed confrontation was less extensive, contact with the English settlers brought economic subjection, debt and servitude. The Native Americans were constantly involved in local conflicts with the colonists over land and hunting rights. Their territories were gradually and inexorably usurped; and trials under English law in colonial courts pronounced them the offenders.[26] Though Pope certainly did not intend to evoke this specific history of suffering, the image of the Native American victim of imperialism is, willy-nilly, a resonant one for him and for his age. A contemporary poem by Richard Savage gives evidence of this resonance from a perspective very different from Pope's:

Do You the neighb'ring blameless *Indian* aid,
Culture what he neglects, not His invade;
Dare not, oh dare not, with ambitious View,
Force or demand Subjection, never due.
Let, by *My* specious Name [Public Spirit] no
    Tyrants rise,
And cry, while they enslave, they civilize!
Know *LIBERTY* and *I* are still the *same*,
Congenial! — ever mingling Flame with Flame!
Why must I *Afric*'s sable Children see

> Vended for Slaves, though form'd by Nature free,
> The nameless Tortures cruel Minds invent,
> Those to subject, whom Nature equal meant?[27]

Thus, while Pope's 'poor Indian' passage seems to provide a sentimental argument for passivity, it advertises, though implicitly, an alternative indication of the oppressive activity of imperial power, an activity of which Savage's parallel 'blameless *Indian*' is well aware. In the quietist context of the *Essay on Man* this implicit alternative, like the recollection of the slavery passage from *Windsor-Forest*, is weird and uneasy, as if the poem's imagery accidentally exposed a threat for which the notion of a beneficient natural order — even if it operates on a general scale and in the long run — cannot account.

The threat of violence is not restricted to the single image of the Indian, though there it takes on its most directly political valence. The *Essay on Man*, strangely like *Windsor-Forest*, returns more than once to the representation of the slaughter of animals.[28] In the first epistle, just before the appearance of the Indian, the poem illustrates the dependence of happiness upon ignorance with a description of another victim:

> The lamb thy riot dooms to bleed to-day,
> Had he thy Reason, would he skip and play?
> Pleas'd to the last, he crops the flow'ry food,
> And licks the hand just rais'd to shed his blood.
>
> (I, 81–4)

And in Epistle III, to define the interconnection of every being in the orderly system of nature, Pope provides a more comic version of the same metaphorical lesson:

> Know, Nature's children all divide her care;
> The fur that warms a monarch, warm'd a bear.
> While Man exclaims, "See all things for my use!"
> "See man for mine!" replies a pamper'd goose.
>
> (III, 43–6)

The doctrine that animals are providentially provided for man's use can be found in contemporary encomia on trade and imperialism, in the notion that the whole order of nature, including climate, winds, the possibilities of navigation and the regional variety of products, is designed to promote commerce and guarantee prosperity.[29] Defoe argues, for instance, that it is through this divine provision that sheep are 'the tamest, quietest, submissivist Creatures in the World, that lay their Throats down to your Knife, and their Backs to the Sheers'.[30] And other writers cite the natural collaboration of birds, tortoises, sables, silkworms, elephants and — perhaps most prominently — whales in supporting a productive commerce.

Pope's images of animals, though ostensibly meant as a caution against human pride, clearly evoke this doctrine of power and acquisition. Beneficent mutual dependency is quickly unmasked here: the animals in the *Essay* devour one another, and man, the model for the 'chain of Love' (III, 7) that holds the system together, devours them all:

> Man cares for all: to birds he gives his woods,
> To beasts his pastures, and to fish his floods;
> For some his Int'rest prompts him to provide,
> For more his pleasure, yet for more his pride:
> All feed on one vain Patron, and enjoy
> Th'extensive blessing of his luxury.
> That very life his learned hunger craves,
> He saves from famine, from the savage saves;
> Nay, feasts the animal he dooms his feast,
> And, 'till he ends the being, makes it blest;
> Which sees no more the stroke, or feels the pain,
> Than favour'd Man by touch etherial slain.
> The creature had his feast of life before;
> Thou too must perish, when thy feast is o'er!
>
> (III, 57—70)

In *Windsor-Forest* the pheasant and the fish, the pastoral victims of imperialism, are in the same relation to man as the *Essay*'s goose, and that earlier poem too wants to see the predatory violence of imperial power as natural and beneficent. But the claim for beneficence in both cases undermines itself, in the *Essay on Man* by invoking a problematic relationship of exploitation as a central positive image.

Imperial exploitation forms a backdrop to the poem in at least one other respect. Pope's renditions of human pride echo the rhetoric of imperialism which we identified in *The Rape of the Lock* and *Windsor-Forest*. In Epistle III he asks:

> Is it for thee the lark ascends and sings?
> Joy tunes his voice, joy elevates his wings:
> Is it for thee the linnet pours his throat?
> Loves of his own and raptures swell the note.
>
> (III, 31—4)

And in the first epistle he renders the same sentiment through ironic direct quotation:

> Ask for what end the heav'nly bodies shine,
> Earth for what use? Pride answers, ' 'Tis for mine:
> 'For me kind Nature wakes her genial pow'r,
> 'Suckles each herb, and spreads out ev'ry flow'r;
> 'Annual for me, the grape, the rose renew
> 'The juice nectareous, and the balmy dew;
> 'For me, the mine a thousand treasures brings;
> 'For me, health gushes from a thousand springs;
> 'Seas roll to waft me, suns to light me rise;
> 'My foot-stool earth, my canopy the skies.'
>
> (I, 131—40)

Pope is here echoing a traditional attack on anthropocentrism,[31] but he is also invoking another contemporary tradition. The 'thousand treasures' recall the 'Unnumber'd Treasures' of Belinda's toilet, and the co-operative stars and seas the universal collaboration of nature in the voyages of discovery. The inverted syntax, which places 'For me' in first position in the line, is identical to Father Thames's climactic claim in *Windsor-Forest*:

> For me the Balm shall bleed, and Amber flow,
> The Coral redden, and the Ruby glow.
>
> (393–4)

In Pope's own immediate past, this rhetoric echoes the conclusion of the *Messiah* (1712), the model for the closing passage of *Windsor-Forest*, in which the glory of Salem (that is, Jerusalem) at Christ's nativity is celebrated as an imperialist prosperity:

> See barb'rous Nations at thy Gates attend,
> Walk in thy Light, and in thy Temple bend.
> See thy bright Altars throng'd with prostrate Kings,
> And heap'd with Products of *Sabæan* Springs!
> For thee, *Idume*'s spicy Forests blow;
> And Seeds of Gold in *Ophyr*'s Mountains glow.
>
> (91–6)

Indeed this locution seems to be a period trope for the pleasures of mercantile accumulation, occurring with notable frequency in the imperialist passages of the minor poetry of the age. In Young's *Imperium·Pelagi* (1729) its connection with the general co-operation of nature is most explicit:

> Luxuriant Isle! What Tide that flows,
> Or Stream that glides, or Wind that blows,
> Or genial Sun that shines, or Show'r that pours,
> But flows, glides, breathes, shines, pours for thee?
> How every Heart dilates to see
> Each Land's each Season blending on thy Shores?
> . . .
> *Britain!* behold the World's wide Face;
> Not cover'd Half with *solid* Space,
> Three Parts are *fluid*; Empire of the Sea!
> And why? for Commerce. *Ocean* Streams
> For *that*, thro' all his various *Names*:
> And if for *Commerce*, *Ocean* flows for Thee.[32]

The structure of initial repetition or anaphora, more common in the heroic couplet versions of the trope, give it even greater rhetorical emphasis. It is repeated seven times in James Ralph's *Clarinda, or the Fair Libertine* (1729):

> For them the Gold is dug on Guinea's Coast,
> And sparkling Gems the farthest Indies boast,
> For them Arabia breathes its spicy Gale,
> And fearless Seamen kill the Greenland Whale.
> For them the Murex yields its purple Dye,
> And orient Pearls in Sea-bred Oisters lye;
> For them, in clouded Shell, the Tortoise shines,
> And huge *Behemoth* his vast Trunk resigns;
> For them, in various Plumes, the Birds are gay,
> And *Sables* bleed, the savage Hunter's Prey!
> For them the *Merchant*, wide to ev'ry Sail,
> Trusts all his Hopes and stretches ev'ry Gale,
> For them, O'er all the World, he dares to roam,
> And safe conveys its gather'd Riches home.[33]

And again in J.D. Breval's *Art of Dress* (1717):

> For you, th'*Italian* Worm her Silk prepares,
> And distant *India* sends her choicest Wares.[34]

And also in Soame Jenyns's *Art of Dancing* (1730):

> For you the silkworms fine-wrought webs display,
> And lab'ring spin their little lives away,
> For you bright gems with radiant colours glow,
> Fair as the dies that paint the heav'nly bow,
> For you the sea resigns its pearly store,
> And earth unlocks her mines of treasur'd ore.[35]

The pronouns in these last three poems refer to the ladies — emblems of cultural expansion — who, like Belinda, are adorned with the commodities of a prosperous mercantilism. Indeed, all these passages — except the second from the *Essay on Man* — betray a systematic effort at displacement from the aggressively acquisitive imperialist subject. Though in every case it is 'me' who desires, 'me' who acquires and 'me' who profits from the goods so glowingly enumerated, either woman or the female

construct of 'Britannia' is made to stand for this desire in
the pronouns 'thee', 'them' and 'you'.

Though the explicit purpose of this imperialist trope in
the Essay on Man is to ridicule anthropocentrism, it carries
with it all the attractions of acquisition and power that we
can easily see in its other contemporary appearances.
Pope's obvious irony cannot negate these attractions,
especially since he has filled his poem with metaphors of
submission from imperialist apologia. The Indian and the
animals serve as images of co-operative quiescence strongly
symptomatic and supportive of an expansionist ideology.
Though the epithets — 'his woods', 'his pastures', 'his
floods' — that describe man's treatment of the animals in
the chain of love satirize the claim to pre-eminence and
point forward to the deflating line 'thou too must perish',
they also supply a generalized advocacy of appropriation,
a fantasy of a perfect hierarchy of exploitation that stands
in uneasy tension with the poem's attacks on pride. From
this perspective, the Essay's message of submission appears
to be built upon an image of power and acquisition, upon
the assumption of a hierarchical system of exploitation. It
is as if the displacement of the desire for acquisition upon
the woman that we discovered in the trope of 'for me'
surfaces in the Essay as a symptomatic affective ambiguity:
the Indian and the sheep do submit 'for me', and their
submission is extolled, but at the same time the poem
preaches against the very appropriation of power that
requires such submission. This ambivalence in the Essay's
treatment of oppression helps to explain the ill-concealed
uneasiness of Pope's least respected line: 'One truth is
clear, "Whatever IS, is RIGHT" ' (I, 294). The blank and
abstract assertiveness of this passage embraces the dichotomy that I have been belabouring here: the exemplary
submission of the Indian to 'Whatever IS' is one thing, and
the sanguine acceptance of an order of oppression by a
prosperous and expanding society is another. In the latter,
'submission' could easily be translated as imperialism.
Pope's optimistic philosophy in the Essay is readily seen as

a defence of the status quo, however brutal or unjust. But the allusions to imperialist ideology that we have uncovered in the poem show that defence to be more coercive and more concrete than a merely passive acceptance of the inevitable.

If we turn now, fortified with our reading of some of the *Essay*'s metaphors, to an analysis of the poem's philosophy, perhaps we will be in a position to evaluate the problem in its logic. The absence of rigour in Pope's philosophical formulations is a familiar focus for attack.[36] But Pope is not our enemy; he is our route to a closer and more complex reading of the major ideologies of the day, and his poems are documents of our own ideological past. The issue for us is not the looseness of Pope's logic — we know he was no philosopher — but the relationship between the symptomatic gaps in his philosophical argument and the affective ambivalence of his poetic language.

Most critiques of the logical coherence of the *Essay on Man* begin with the second epistle and its theory of human nature. The first epistle serves mainly to introduce the basic scheme of the poem — the great chain of being — and the notions of order, hierarchy and harmony that we found associated with the cosmic order of nature in the *Essay on Criticism*. Here again Pope is reworking, though with more complexity and elaboration, motifs deriving from Renaissance neo-Platonic thought. All creation exists in a hierarchy where everything has its proper place and 'All must full or not coherent be' (I, 45) — every conceivable place, from inanimate objects to God, is and must be filled.[37] Nothing can move out of its place on the chain, for such a transgression would disrupt the structure of the universe and result in chaos:

Let Earth unbalanc'd from her orbit fly,
Planets and Suns run lawless thro' the sky,
Let ruling Angels from their spheres be hurl'd,
Being on being wreck'd, and world on world.

(I, 251–4)

Everything in this 'Vast chain of being' (I, 237) is thus mutually dependent and, though hierarchical, divinely harmonious. When Pope outlines this scheme and places man in structural relationship with the rest of creation, his position is simple and consistent. When he begins to elaborate the system in the second epistle, however, he produces a series of inconsistencies that inform the rest of the poem.

Epistle II could be described as logically diffuse. Though it is possible, through an explanation and elaboration of Pope's categories, to argue for coherence in Pope's presentation of the relationship of reason and passion or self-love and virtue,[38] the system as it stands in the poem is at best unsteady, at worst incoherent. The most often-cited problem is the shifting role of reason. We are presented at first with a clear opposition: 'What Reason weaves, by Passion is undone' (II, 42). Reason and passion are the two competing principles of human nature, each with a separate role: 'Nor this a good, nor that a bad we call,/Each works its end, to move or govern all' (II, 55–6). But this clear duality is quickly and confusingly over-complicated. On the one hand reason, the comparing principle, 'rules the whole' (II, 60); in accordance with nature, reason should subject and confine the passions (II, 115–20). On the other hand, passion seems the pre-dominant force: 'Reason itself but gives it edge and pow'r' (II, 147). Reason is a 'weak queen' (II, 150), directed by passion, the usurping 'fav'rite' whom we 'wretched subjects' obey (II, 149–50). In fact reason can supply no 'arms' for the battle with passion, it is 'helpless', pleading, 'no guide' (II, 151–62), and it only strengthens the ruling passion by eliminating weaker ones (II, 158). This state of affairs is both unfortunate and desirable.

The problem with reason and passion is connected with the use of the theory of the ruling passion in the epistle, and the related appearance of virtue in conjunction with the notion of self-love. The turn from a balanced opposi-tion of reason and passion to a comparative privileging of passion as a more determinant category accords with the rise in the argument of the efficacious notion of the ruling passion. That is, since the theory of the ruling passion is clearly designed to account for the ultimately beneficent order of the 'state of man', both as an individual and, later, in respect to society, then passion must be granted a larger significance than a simple opposition with reason would permit. The usurpation of reason by passion begins with the designation of the passions as modes of self-love, since reason is also implicitly defined as simply a long-term form of the same motivating force (II, 71—2, 93—6). The next major ambiguity in the epistle arises precisely here, in the assignment of virtue to either reason or self-love. Virtue is clearly an essential ingredient of any scheme of beneficent order, and, not surprisingly, in a system where the relation of reason and passion is elusive, virtue can be found in either camp. On the one hand, it seems to be potentially separable from self-love; it arises from passions of 'fair means' that therefore come under the care of reason and, 'that imparted, court a nobler aim,/Exalt their kind, and take some Virtue's name' (II, 97—100).[39] On the other hand, it is grafted onto the ruling passion by the 'Eternal Art' that educes 'good from ill' (II, 175—6). In this guise, it is much more clearly constituted by self-love; it cannot claim to take a separate course or pursue a 'nobler aim', and it is characterized, in the succeeding examples, by a virtual simultaneity with vice, which we shall shortly examine.

But this simultaneity is another *locus* of anxiety in the epistle, another source of potential ambiguity. The notion of a 'nobler aim' or separate end for virtue persists in Pope's affirmation of a clear and diametrical moral distinction: 'Vice is a monster of so frightful mien,/As, to be hated, needs but to be seen' (II, 217—18). The difference between vice and virtue is as clear as 'black and white': 'Ask your own heart, and nothing is so plain;/'Tis to mistake them, costs the time and pain' (II, 214—16). But, on the other hand, virtue is so intermingled with vice that 'the diff'rence is too nice/Where ends the Virtue, or begins the Vice' (II, 209—10). Again, the terms can be adjusted and the difficulty mitigated so as to produce a reading that emphasizes not incoherence but rather Pope's 'disposition to combine and adapt ideas'.[40] He certainly had such a disposition, and he deliberately treads a thin line in the *Essay* in an effort to bring together disparate positions. But it is this very disposition and this thin line that we must examine. The purpose of my reading of the *Essay on Man* is not to reconcile contradiction but to define the strong poles of the poem, in order to assess their relevance to its ideology.

The slippages that we have so far located primarily in the second epistle of the *Essay* are as complex and intricate as the disparate traditions — Christian and classical — that stand behind the poem's philosophical categories. But the crucial problem for Pope lies in the relatively simple question of the definition of virtue in relation to self-interest. We can pursue this problem further if we move from Epistle II to the descriptions of virtue in the rest of the poem. On the one hand, as we have begun to see, the *Essay* argues that virtues are the products of the passions — of anger, avarice, sloth and lust:

> The surest Virtues thus from Passions shoot,
> Wild Nature's vigor working at the root.
> What crops of wit and honesty appear
> From spleen, from obstinacy, hate, or fear!
> See anger, zeal and fortitude supply;
> Ev'n av'rice, prudence; sloth, philosophy;
> Lust, thro' some certain strainers well refin'd,
> Is gentle love, and charms all womankind:
> Envy, to which th'ignoble mind's a slave,
> Is emulation in the learn'd or brave:
> Nor Virtue, male or female, can we name,
> But what will grow on Pride, or grow on Shame.
>
> (II, 183—94)

Nature operates so that man's ruling passion acts 'in one

interest' with his best principles (II, 176–80) and thereby generates his best actions. Self-interest thus serves mankind by producing appropriate 'vices' in their proper places:

> Shame to the virgin, to the matron pride,
> Fear to the statesman, rashness to the chief,
> To kings presumption, and to crowds belief,
> That Virtue's ends from Vanity can raise,
> Which seeks no int'rest, no reward but praise;
> And build on wants, and on defects of mind,
> The joy, the peace, the glory of Mankind.
>
> (II, 242–8)

In this proto-utilitarian view, virtue is defined in terms of results, in terms of one's acts in the world, and not in terms of altruism or the abstract principles of moral 'rigorism'.[41] But the *Essay* offers the opposite position as well: in Epistle II, as we have seen, virtues are, if only briefly, noble passions that 'Exalt their kind' (II, 100) and can be clearly discriminated from vice. And in Epistle IV virtue is:

> The only point where human bliss stands still,
> And tastes the good without the fall to ill;
> Where only Merit constant pay receives,
> Is blest in what it takes, and what it gives;
> The joy unequal'd, if its end it gain,
> And if it lose, attended with no pain:
> Without satiety, tho' e'er so blest,
> And but more relish'd as the more distress'd:
> The broadest mirth unfeeling Folly wears,
> Less pleasing far than Virtue's very tears.
> Good, from each object, from each place acquir'd,
> For ever exercis'd, yet never tir'd;
> Never elated, while one man's oppress'd;
> Never dejected, while another's bless'd;
> And where no wants, no wishes can remain,
> Since but to wish more Virtue, is to gain.
>
> (IV, 311–26)

The virtuous person, then, is one 'Who noble ends by noble means obtains,/Or failing, smiles in exile or in chains' (IV, 233—4). He chooses right or wrong (IV, 86), is charitable and benevolent, and sets no store by wealth, rank, greatness, fame or parts (IV, 185—268). The reward of virtue is happiness, 'The soul's calm sun-shine, and the heart-felt joy' (IV, 168), a kind of earthly bliss derived from the sensibility of doing good. This sort of virtue, needless to say, is not to be found in the 'wickedly wise' or 'madly brave' (IV, 231): the rash chief, then, who served to exemplify virtue in Epistle II, is explicitly excluded here in favour of those with more altruistic motives and more ascetic ideals.

We can pursue this basic dichotomy in a variety of directions. First, we can use it to account for other inconsistencies in the poem. The problem that we have already noted in the role of reason as a force either opposing or abetting the passions is a consequence of this larger difficulty. If there are separate 'good' and 'bad' passions in the human mind, then Pope must posit a controlling reason that can set them in order. But if the passions in general are in action transmuted into virtues, the only role for reason is co-operative. In addition, the problematic distinction in the *Essay* between 'passions' on the one hand and 'vice' and 'virtue' on the other also belongs to the basic dichotomy that we have identified. If virtue comes from the good results of vicious passions in action, then there is no inherent distinction between virtue and vice: in a sense virtues are vices. But the poem persistently claims to distinguish vice from virtue, and, as we have already noticed, Pope attacks self-interest in the form of error, presumption, pride, imperfection and vanity throughout the *Essay*.[42]

This problem is translated into social terms in the third Epistle: '*Of the Nature and State of* Man, *with respect to* Society'. Here Pope provides two models for the origin of society, in a pseudo-historical relationship with one another. The first posits an order based on 'the chain of love' (III, 7), in which man, naturally good, learns through his love for the opposite sex and for the young to love all of creation. This process produces the initial social bond. In the other scheme, presented as a second phase in primitive history,[43] social order is predicated upon the social contract, by which warring individuals concede some of their immediate self-interest in order to guarantee their long-term safety:

> So drives Self-love, thro' just and thro' unjust,
> To one Man's pow'r, ambition, lucre, lust:
> The same Self-love, in all, becomes the cause
> Of what restrains him, Government and Laws.
> For, what one likes if others like as well,
> What serves one will, when many wills rebel?
> How shall he keep, what, sleeping or awake,
> A weaker may surprise, a stronger take?
> His safety must his liberty restrain:
> All join to guard what each desires to gain.
> Forc'd into virtue thus by Self-defence,
> Ev'n Kings learn'd justice and benevolence:
> Self-love forsook the path it first pursu'd,
> And found the private in the public good.
>
> (III, 269–82)

In the first scheme, virtue is a positive attribute derived from instinctual love. In the second, it arises from self-defence. Again, the fundamental issue is whether the beneficence of nature that the poem posits and sets out at its opening to 'vindicate' derives from consequences or motives, whether God is good because man's self-interest operates — despite his intentions — to good ends or because man is naturally and instinctively loving, whether virtue is utilitarian or absolute.

Not surprisingly, the vision of human life that the *Essay* presents is also infected by this dichotomy. On the one hand, the poem glories in the enlightened soul that transcends the trivial and sees beyond the concrete to a broader realm of self-knowledge and altruism:

> For him alone, Hope leads from goal to goal,
> And opens still, and opens on his soul,
> 'Till lengthen'd on to Faith, and unconfin'd,
> It pours the bliss that fills up all the mind.
> He sees, why Nature plants in Man alone
> Hope of known bliss, and Faith in bliss unknown:
> (Nature, whose dictates to no other kind
> Are giv'n in vain, but what they seek they find)
> Wise is her present; she connects in this
> His greatest Virtue with his greatest Bliss,
> At once his own bright prospect to be blest,
> And strongest motive to assist the rest.
>
> (IV, 341–52)

But on the other hand, the poem sees human life as empty, meaningless, and vain:

> Behold the child, by Nature's kindly law,
> Pleas'd with a rattle, tickled with a straw:
> Some livelier play-thing gives his youth delight,
> A little louder, but as empty quite:
> Scarfs, garters, gold, amuse his riper stage;
> And beads and pray'r-books are the toys of age:
> Pleas'd with this bauble still, as that before;
> 'Till tir'd he sleeps, and Life's poor play is o'er!
>
> (II, 275–82)

In both passages nature is the beneficent agent of man's fate, but in the first version the effect of nature is to broaden and brighten human prospects, to raise man through hope and faith to a better understanding of his condition. In the second, 'Nature's kindly law' can only keep man entertained for the brief tenure of his oblivious mortality. Each of these views is warranted in the work's 'philosophy': the former based on the notion of a categorical morality defined through implicit acceptance of the chain of love, the latter on a proto-utilitarian ethic emphasizing the effects of self-love as it operates in the world.[44]

With this last example of the images of human life

generated by the *Essay*'s contradictory treatment of virtue and passion, we have already returned to the point at which we began our discussion, the problem of the poem's effect. Where does the ambivalence of its imagery — the evocation of exploitation, the rhetoric of imperialism, the incongruous echoes of *Windsor-Forest* — meet the incoherence of its philosophical system? Albert O. Hirschman has suggested that the transformation of the idea of the passions from a destructive force to be repressed or controlled into a positive force to be harnessed or managed for the benefit of the public welfare coincided with the development of capitalism and served in the eighteenth century as a major political argument in favour of the new economic system.[45] One version of this new notion is summarized by Giambattista Vico:

> Legislation considers man as he is in order to turn him to good uses in human society. Out of ferocity, avarice and ambition, the three vices which run throughout the human race, it creates the military, merchant and governing classes, and thus the strength, riches and wisdom of commonwealths. Out of these three great vices, which would certainly destroy all mankind on the face of the earth, it makes civil happiness.
>
> This axiom proves that there is divine providence and further that it is a divine legislative mind. For out of the passions of men each bent on his private advantage, for the sake of which they would live like wild beasts in the wilderness, it has made the civil orders by which they may live in human society.[46]

We may recall here Pope's 'Fear to the statesman, rashness to the chief/To kings presumption, and to crowds belief' (II, 243–4). In England, Addison gives a similar though more circumscribed definition of the positive social value of the passions:

> The Soul, considered abstractedly from its Passions, is of a remiss and sedentary Nature, slow in its Resolves,

and languishing in its Executions. The use therefore of the Passions, is to stir it up and put it upon Action, to awaken the Understanding, to enforce the Will, and to make the whole Man more vigorous and attentive in the Prosecution of his Designs. As this is the End of the Passions in general, so it is particularly of Ambition, which pushes the Soul to such Actions as are apt to procure Honour and Reputation to the Actor. But if we carry our Reflections higher, we may discover further Ends of Providence in implanting this Passion in Mankind.

It was necessary for the World, that Arts should be invented and improved, Books written and transmitted to Posterity, Nations conquered and civilized: Now since the proper and genuine Motives to these and the like great Actions, would only influence vertuous Minds; there would be but small Improvements in the World, were there not some common Principle of Action working equally with all Men. And such a Principle is Ambition or a Desire of Fame, by which great Endowments are not suffered to lie idle and useless to the Publick, and many vicious Men over-reached, as it were, and engaged contrary to their natural Inclinations in a glorious and laudable course of Action.[47]

Addison's statement indicates the positive conjunction of imperialism, arts and self-interest in the thinking of the period. This is the same interdependency that we have been approaching in our discussion of the role of imperialist apologia in Pope's paean to the beneficent universal efficacy of self-interest.

In the process of the transformation of the passions' place in political, ethical and psychological thought, traditional Christian vices — avarice, pride and especially luxury — came to be seen as social virtues by which, ultimately, money-making, competition, expansion, acquisition, accumulation and prosperity were promoted.

The new 'virtues' that this reasoning discovered in the passions were often linked to 'interest', which was inserted into the scheme either as a set of countervailing passions by which wilder and more aggressive ones could be balanced, or, in a less morally radical move, as a kind of forethinking equivalent of passion that could direct its social utility. In Pope, we see the influence of the former theory most clearly in the description of self-interest in the social scheme of Epistle III, where, in a musical metaphor typical of images of *concordia discors*,

> . . . jarring int'rests of themselves create
> Th'according music of a well-mix'd State.
>
> (III, 293—4)

And we can locate the latter theory in those later passages of Epistle II where reason takes a subordinate role in relation to passion or seems to be defined as a version of more far-seeing self-interest.

The best-known English exponent of these views is Pope's contemporary Bernard Mandeville, who posits a whole system of public prosperity based upon private vices in his *Fable of the Bees: Or, Private Vices, Publick Benefits* (1705—29). Mandeville's work is based on the paradoxical observation that, contrary to traditional theories of social prosperity where the good of the state was directly equated with individual virtue, the prosperity of the complex modern state seems necessarily to be based on private vice:

> THE Root of Evil, Avarice,
> That damn'd ill-natur'd baneful Vice,
> Was Slave to Prodigality,
> That Noble Sin; whilst Luxury
> Employ'd a Million of the Poor,
> And odious Pride a Million more:
> Envy it self, and Vanity,
> Were Ministers of Industry;
> Their darling Folly, Fickleness,

> In Diet, Furniture and Dress,
> That strange ridic'lous Vice, was made
> The very Wheel, that turn'd the Trade.
> . . .
>
>   THUS Vice nurs'd Ingenuity,
> Which join'd with Time and Industry,
> Had carry'd Life's Conveniencies,
> It's real Pleasures, Comforts, Ease,
> To such a Height, the very Poor
> Liv'd better than the Rich before,
> And nothing could be added more.[48]

Mandeville found this scheme both socially necessary and morally abhorrent, and he used his position as a means of attacking both the immorality of modern society and the categorical and abstract principles of traditional moralists. Significantly, in the manuscript version of the *Essay on Man*, Pope included what seems like a direct reference to Mandeville:

> But HEAV'N'S great view is One, and that the Whole:
> That counter-works each folly and caprice;
> And public good extracts from private vice.
>
> (II, 238–40)[49]

While Pope is not simply imitating Mandeville, and while Mandeville is not the sole or even perhaps the most significant influence on the *Essay*, the philosophical tensions and inconsistencies that we have found in the poem are structurally similar to the famous ethical paradox of Mandeville's work. F.B. Kaye summarizes Mandeville's problem this way:

> By juxtaposing together the utilitarian principles by which the world is inevitably controlled and the demands of rigoristic ethics, and showing their irreconcilability, Mandeville achieved a latent *reductio ad absurdum* of the rigoristic point of view. But he never educed this *reductio ad absurdum*. Although he spent most of his book in the demonstration that a

life regulated by the principles of rigoristic virtue as expressed in his definition is not only impossible but highly undesirable, whereas the actual immoral world is a pleasant place, he continued to announce the sanctity of the rigoristic creed. This paradoxical ethical duet which Mandeville carried on with himself is the point to note here, for it is this fact which gives the clue to the influence on ethics which he exerted.[50]

The Fable of the Bees struggles — though in a very different mode and manner — with the same contradiction as the *Essay on Man*. The precedent for Pope is in the structure of that 'ethical duet'.

Philosophically, then, the *Essay on Man* hangs between a capitalist ethic and traditional Christian morality. In fact, it documents in its own contradictions the appropriation of the passions by a new ideological system. As we have seen, the poem alternately supports a proto-utilitarian and a rigoristic moral understanding of virtue, and it defines man and his role in society in terms of both aggressive self-interest and Christian selflessness. It is no accident, then, though perhaps no conscious plan, that the poem refers back to the period's most resonant apology for expansion and acquisition, *Windsor-Forest*. This fundamental indecision in its theoretical structure begins to explain why, in its metaphorical structure, the *Essay on Man* is predicated on the problematic fantasy of an ideal exploitation; why it seems to warn against a system that it advocates; why it appears unable to distinguish beneficence from oppression, benevolence from threat, consolation from violence: why the Indian and the lamb place such a strain on the exhortation to 'Submit'; and why the phrase 'Whatever IS, is RIGHT', to the extent that it translates that neo-Platonic chain of being into a chain of capitalist exploitation, fails to carry even an internal conviction of efficacy.

We can read the *Essay on Man* in a variety of ways, depending on where we place the poem in the dynamic of eighteenth-century history. From a progressive perspective,

we can see it as an early, tentative and therefore in-
complete formulation of capitalist ideology. From a
reactionary perspective, it could be said to embody the
struggle against capitalist hegemony, the incoherence of
its treatment of the passions standing as a testament to
Pope's resistance to the arguments for an acquisitive self-
interest. But perhaps we can best appreciate its significance
if we read it at the same time in both ways. In *The Wealth
of Nations* (1776), the work that represents the great
culmination of the theory of passion and self-interest,
Adam Smith expresses a strangely familiar ambivalence
toward the system for which he is the century's major
theorist. His sense of the positive and self-sufficient role
of self-interest in producing progress and social welfare
becomes one of the central tenets of his economic theory:

> The natural effort of every individual to better his
> own condition, when suffered to exert itself with
> freedom and security, is so powerful a principle, that
> it is alone, and without any assistance, not only
> capable of carrying on the society to wealth and
> prosperity, but of surmounting a hundred impertinent
> obstructions with which the folly of human laws too
> often encumbers its operations.[51]

But Adam Smith also saw the system of free self-interest
that he supported as corrupting, degrading and destructive
of traditional values. In *The Wealth of Nations* his
advocacy of the division of labour, which he defines as an
essential component for economic prosperity, is notoriously
problematized and undercut:

> [The labourer] has no occasion to exert his under-
> standing, or to exercise his invention. . . . He naturally
> . . . becomes as stupid and ignorant as it is possible
> for a human creature to become. The torpor of his
> mind renders him, not only incapable of relishing or
> bearing a part in any rational conversation, but of
> conceiving any generous, noble, or tender sentiment.[52]

Elsewhere Smith addresses the effects of capitalism in a broader context: 'These are the disadvantages of a commercial spirit. The minds of men are contracted, and rendered incapable of elevation. Education is despised, or at least neglected, and heroic spirit is almost utterly extinguished.'[53] 'Life's poor play' is here confronted in its most degraded aspect. The sad irony of Smith's position — its double stance of advocacy and regret, and even its futile reference backwards to a pre-capitalist 'heroic spirit' — enables us to recover the much obscurer poignancy and paradox of the *Essay on Man*'s 'ethical duet'.

3   The Ideology of Neo-Classical Aesthetics:
    Epistles to Several Persons (1731–5)

We know from the Advertisement to the 'death-bed' edition of the *Epistles to Several Persons* that Pope saw a direct connection between these poems and the *Essay on Man*.[1] Together they were to frame Pope's *opus magnum*, a discursive epic on humankind conceived as a dilated version of the *Essay on Man*. That longer and evidently uncompletable work was, according to Pope's prospectus, to begin with the four epistles of the *Essay on Man*, and to move on to a book on reason, science, learning and their misuses, a book on civil government, and a book on private ethics. As Pope himself indicates, this scheme follows the outline of the four epistles of the *Essay on Man* — beginning with the limits of human reason in respect to the universe and in respect to man himself, and moving to society, and finally to individual virtue. The *Epistles to Several Persons*, then, along with other similar moral essays, were to constitute that last book on private morality, the conclusion of Pope's major philosophical/poetic effort. These poems, like the *Essay on Man*, seek to place traditional definitions of character and morality, vice and virtue, in a capitalist context. Their struggle with the status of ethics in an impersonal economic system, with the nature of moral value in the new world of the commodity, reflect the central underlying obsession of Pope's *opus magnum*: the attempt to provide a cultural, ethical and psychological rationale — both critical and descriptive — for a capitalist mode of production.

We have already begun to see the inherent problems of Pope's project in our examination of the imagistic ambivalences and the dual ethical allegiances of the *Essay on Man*. The *Epistles to Several Persons* will offer further evidence of this 'ethical duet'. They will also provide a perspective on the place of the 'characters of women' in the problematic of Pope's poetry, and an indication of the role of pastoral scene-painting in Pope's ethical project. Perhaps this constellation of ruling problems — ethical, sexual and pastoral — will give us some grounds for guessing why Pope's *opus magnum* could not be written.

I

Epistle I, *To Cobham* (1734) centres upon the same ambivalent theories of character that we observed in the problematic assertions of the *Essay on Man*; only here that ambivalence is thematized primarily in the difficulty of knowing and located in the indecision of the observer:

> To Observations which ourselves we make,
> We grow more partial for th' observer's sake.
>
> (11–12)

From the opening lines of the poem, the attempt to construct a system for understanding and defining character is entangled with the problem of the status of man's knowledge of his fellow men, and this complexity itself is seen as a result of the elusiveness of character:

> . . . the diff'rence is as great between
> The optics seeing, as the objects seen.
> All Manners take a tincture from our own,
> Or some discolour'd thro' our Passions shown.
>
> (23–6)

In other words, if the complexity and inaccessibility of

motives make human character difficult to determine, those very qualities in the observer's character necessarily compound the problem. And indeed the first section of the poem, which elaborates the uncertain state of our knowledge about human character, systematically conflates observer and observed: 'you' and 'he' are merged in 'us' — 'our depths', 'our shallows', 'our spring of action' (29, 42).

From this opening declaration of the problem of knowing, the poem goes on to reject the judgement of character based on the congruence of action and motive:

> In vain the Sage, with retrospective eye,
> Would from th'apparent What conclude the Why,
> Infer the Motive from the Deed, and shew,
> That what we chanc'd was what we meant to do.
>
> (51—4)

What we do, good or bad, may in fact be motivated by some form of self-interest:

> Not always Actions shew the man: we find
> Who does a kindness, is not therefore kind,
> Perhaps Prosperity becalm'd his breast,
> Perhaps the Wind just shifted from the east:
> Not therefore humble he who seeks retreat,
> Pride guides his steps, and bids him shun the great:
> Who combats bravely is not therefore brave,
> He dreads a death-bed like the meanest slave:
> Who reasons wisely is not therefore wise,
> His pride in Reas'ning, not in Acting lies.
>
> (61—70)

This poem does not go as far as the *Essay on Man* towards suggesting explicitly that traditional 'vice' produces social 'virtue' and public welfare, but these examples accord with that argument. The man who 'does a kindness' may be motivated by private 'Prosperity', which is the source of public peace in *Windsor-Forest* and one of the period's strongest rationalizations for mercantile expansion. And if prosperity can make man kind, pride can make him humble and cowardice can make him brave. In fact, self-interest seems to reign supreme in the tone and the specific examples of this poem. There are no strong images of disinterested behaviour in the epistle, no 'nobler aims'. A 'Hero' may 'turn a crafty Knave' because he 'was sick, in love, or had not din'd' (78–80). All of us are, according to 'honest Nature', 'Consistent in our follies and our sins' (226–7).

How can we understand character if we have no access to motive except the general assumption of self-interest? Only through observing men's actions in the world, only, that is, by granting the proto-utilitarian premise 'that Actions best discover man' (72). But this premise too is conditional. Pope goes on to argue that actions are, in practice, too varied or too dependent upon context to provide firm evidence in judging human character: deeds may be disparate and inconsistent, rank and education may affect inherent qualities, context may shape men's responses. His conclusion about the possibility of firm judgement is not hopeful:

> Judge we by Nature? Habit can efface,
> Int'rest o'ercome, or Policy take place:
> By Actions? those Uncertainty divides:
> By Passions? these Dissimulation hides:
> Opinions? they still take a wider range:
> Find, if you can, in what you cannot change.
>
> (168–73)

All that remains is change, in observer and observed. The opening survey of the possibilities for understanding the characters of men leaves the poem with little to go on. The sage's failure to infer motives from actions signals the irrelevance of categorical morality, and the variability of human actions makes them useless for the understanding of character. At this point, the poem is asking a question that, on its own terms, cannot be answered: the question of how to supply a determinate and static definition of

character, based on traditional abstract principles of inherent vice and virtue, to a world where the underlying
motivation of all acts is implicitly located in private and
self-interested passions. Indeed, this is a deliberate
dilemma, staged by Pope to exemplify the poem's
dominant premise of the inadequacy of human knowledge.

The conclusion of *To Cobham* unconsciously echoes the
ethical indeterminacies that we have been tracing in the
first half of the poem, tying them to the paradigmatic case
of patriotism. The epistle ends with a list of examples of
self-interest — significantly, a list made up primarily of
Christian vices: lust in the 'rev'rend sire', Helluo's comic
gluttony, miserliness in the 'frugal Crone', vanity, flattery,
avarice and, finally, Cobham's passion of patriotism:

> 'I give and I devise, (old Euclio said,
> And sigh'd) 'My lands and tenements to Ned.'
> Your money, Sir; 'My money, Sir, what all?
> 'Why, — if I must — (then wept) I give it Paul.'
> The Manor, Sir? — 'The Manor! hold,' he cry'd,
> 'Not that, — I cannot part with that' — and dy'd.
>   And you! brave COBHAM, to the latest breath
> Shall feel your ruling passion strong in death:
> Such in those moments as in all the past,
> 'Oh, save my Country, Heav'n!' shall be your last.
>
> (256–65)

There is no doubt that Pope intended the conclusion of
the poem as a compliment, or that he meant Cobham to
stand as an emblem of moral virtue. Cobham wrote to
thank Pope for the 'publick testimony of your esteem and
friendship'.[2] And after his death his widow had these last
two couplets inscribed on a memorial pillar at Stowe. But
how do we know Cobham from the 'rev'rend sire', Helluo
or 'old Euclio'? How do we distinguish the inherent moral
value of one passion over the next, especially when all
actions are generated by universal self-interest?[3] In placing
the good patriot Cobham at the end of that catalogue, the
poem formally conflates him with the examples of vice

that so vividly go before. Indeed this concluding list enacts the earlier thesis that all acts derive from passions and that all passions are evaluatively equivalent, neither virtuous nor vicious except in terms of their benefit to society. The results of Cobham's particular passion may be more beneficial, but its inherent worth and Cobham's inherent virtue, at least on the basis of Pope's previous argument, are no different from the rest. The issue of the passion of patriotism arises again in the *Epistle to Bathurst* (1733), written earlier than *To Cobham* and perhaps influential upon the composition of that poem, especially in its concluding satiric portraits.[4] One of the prominent characters in *To Bathurst* is young Cotta, the patriot who gives his whole estate for 'his Country's love' (212) and receives no reward. This example is offered not as an indication of inherent virtue, but as a signal of the amoral operations of heaven's law, by which extremes in human passions produce a general welfare. Cotta's amorality suggests that Cobham too cannot be seen as a pure and simple example of traditional virtue, the cornerstone of a determinate definition of character. Indeed, patriotism, as the prototype of a stable individual ethics, seems to have a special prominence in the moral problematic of the *opus magnum*: it serves as the emblem both of private virtue and, sometimes simultaneously, of the beneficial public effects of the passions. It plays this pivotal role in *To Cobham*. Though Pope claims in the last lines of that poem to have rediscovered categorical morality, the structure of his conclusion says that no such categories can be distinguished.[5]

Pope's attempt to justify a categorical morality is initiated at the turning point of the epistle with the line 'Search then the Ruling Passion' (174). The ruling passion supplies a systematic means of tying motives to actions, granting the predominance of self-interest. Thus Wharton's 'Lust of Praise' generates both his public eloquence and his private profligacy. And Caesar's ambition even explains the secondary passion of lust that caused him to make 'a noble

dame a whore' (213). The ruling passion repudiates the
paradox of the first half of the epistle, and consequently
the thematization of the doubtful role of the observer in
judging human character fades from the poem when this
claim to resolution is made. Now we can know all:

> . . . There, alone,
> The Wild are constant, and the Cunning known;
> The Fool consistent, and the False sincere;
> Priests, Princes, Women, no dissemblers here.
>
> (174—7)

In fact all we can do is discriminate among kinds of self-
interest. But Pope passes off this discrimination as a
determination of abstract principles of vice and virtue, as a
means to an absolute ethical judgement of character. In
other words, though the ruling passion may solve the
problem of evaluating the relation between action and
motive, it does not warrant the assumption that we can
designate one passion virtuous and one vicious; indeed it
directly opposes that assumption in its systematic levelling
of moral distinctions. The failure of the ruling passion to
provide a means of moral evaluation, and especially the
peculiar parallelism of Cobham with the figures of vice in
the poem's conclusion, all counter Pope's attempt to
supply a neat moral resolution.

The 'ethical duet' that we found in the *Essay on Man* is
thus even more of a duet in *To Cobham*, where it finds its
focus in the problem of determinate character and
personal morality. J.G.A. Pocock has suggested that the
social thinking of the eighteenth century is characterized
by a major implicit debate 'between virtue and passion,
land and commerce, republic and empire, value and
history'. One of the consequences of this debate, according
to Pocock, was that 'social morality was becoming
divorced from personal morality, and from the ego's
confidence in its own integrity and reality.'[6] We can
situate *To Cobham* — and indeed all of these *Epistles* — at
the centre of this ideological paradox. In different ways,

each of them moves between the poles of virtue and passion, calling into question the foundations of personality itself, repeatedly staging the irresolvable contradiction between a cognitively stable, ethically absolute valuation and a contingent social and historical dynamic.

II

Epistle II, *To a Lady* (1735), the last published of the *Epistles to Several Persons*, has been read as a systematic parallel to the *Epistle to Cobham*.[7] It begins, like *To Cobham*, by introducing the premise of the changeableness of human character, which it proceeds to elaborate in its long central section. It turns near its conclusion to the efficacious category of the ruling passion, which serves as the basis for a final generalization. And it ends with a predictable but in some respects extraneous tribute to the exemplary character to whom the epistle is addressed. These structural similarities might lead us to expect to read the poems in the same way, but strangely enough, as we shall find, their effects and assumptions are substantially different. The failure of the parallelism is sex-linked. In applying his paradoxical theory of human character to the 'softer Man' (272), Pope makes women the scapegoats of his ideological dilemma. The misogyny of the poem can be directly linked to this problematic.

Though the *Epistle to a Lady* emphasizes change, it does not take the position of uncertainty and indeterminacy that we found in the *Epistle to Cobham*. In that poem human changeableness renders the sage incapable of judgment. In *To a Lady* female changeability is the basis for extended satiric condemnation. This epistle begins with an assertion of its own access to truth:

Nothing so true as what you once let fall,
'Most Women have no Characters at all.'
                                                    (1–2)

And it repeats this claim in the succeeding lines:

> How many Pictures of one Nymph we view,
> All how unlike each other, all how true!
>
> (5—6)

This poem has no self-doubt. Exhaustively certain of its judgements, it will 'Catch' and 'paint' (20, 16) the changing faces of womankind despite their shifting appearance. Where *To Cobham* generates contradiction, *To a Lady* remains, at least on its own terms, coherent. In *To Cobham* the introduction of the theory of the ruling passion repudiates the indeterminacy that the poem proposes in its first half. In *To a Lady* the ruling passion is ill-prepared for by the demonstration of changeability that occupies the body of the poem, but once asserted, it fits smoothly with the confident attack on female character that precedes it. In other words, *To a Lady* readily accommodates itself to the application of a notion of systematic moral and characterological discrimination, while *To Cobham* cannot ever fully reconcile its position of uncertainty with the sudden advocacy of absolute judgement.

How can poems with such similar premises produce such different effects? It is tempting, and only somewhat unjust, to argue that *To a Lady* is less incoherent and more secure in its judgments than *To Cobham* because the one thing Pope knows in a changeable world is that women are contemptible.[8] But we can go much further in accounting for Pope's misogyny. First, we can discover connections between the attack on women in this poem and Pope's ideological allegiance to classical authority. Second, we can understand the poem as an inverted consequence of the Mandevillian ethic with which Pope struggles in *To Cobham* as well as the *Essay on Man*. And third, we can even link the poem to the representation of commodity fetishism that we found most fully developed in *The Rape of the Lock*.

Pope's misogyny does not spring fully grown from his own personal antagonisms. Classical attacks on women, especially Juvenal's misogynist satires, serve as authority and justification for much of the anti-female literature of Pope's period. In the case of *To a Lady*, classical precedent provides not a specific model, but a context or series of customary tropes through which the criticism of women can be expressed. Ancient Roman misogyny emphasizes dressing, cosmetics, luxury and the implicit relationship of such forms of duplicity and concupiscence to sexuality. These are the themes that we identified in a much less hostile version in Belinda's connection with the products of mercantile expansion in *The Rape of the Lock*. For Pope, as for Juvenal, women embody the material consequences of commodification much more directly than men. Dress and make-up are the outward signs of female falseness derived from a commodified culture, but the direct association of women with the commodity and all its corollaries of indiscriminacy and acquisition also serves to attach an abstract imputation of moral indiscriminacy and deceit to female character. In other words, the capriciousness and inconstancy of women in satiric convention has the same source as their addiction to make-up and appearance. As the privileged locus for the display of the products of accumulation, women dress themselves in the commodities that expansionist culture provides; their duplicity — in *To a Lady* their changeableness — is simply an abstraction from this basic cultural tenet. Thus, as we observed in our discussion of the anthropocentric imperialist trope 'for me', the period's obsession with acquisition, luxury and accumulation is systematically displaced onto women, private figures technically unconnected with the public enterprises of trade and business, who thus become the displaced focus of the attack on a commodified society. It is no coincidence, then, that Pope's misogyny should have such a clear precedent in classical Latin literature. The precedent supplies Pope with an authoritative origin; it supplies us with an initial indication of this poem's ideological connection with mercantile capitalism.

In *To Cobham*, as in the *Essay on Man*, the problem of
the determination of character arises for Pope with the
positing of a separation between inner motives and outer
actions, between private and public realms. The impossi-
bility of probing true motives, the evaluative disjunction of
motives and actions, the Mandevillian vision of a social
utility produced by the self-centred effects of the passions,
and the implicit attack on a coherent theory of virtue, all
are part of the developing notion of a private sphere dis-
continuous with and therefore separate from public life.
The theory of the characters of men in the *Essay on Man*
and the *Epistle to Cobham* is contradictory because, as we
have seen, both those poems begin to acknowledge but
ultimately refuse to accept the division of private from
public virtue. Significantly, *To a Lady* does not confront
this problem:

> But grant, in Public Men sometimes are shown,
> A Woman's seen in Private life alone:
> Our bolder Talents in full light display'd;
> Your Virtues open fairest in the shade.
> Bred to disguise, in Public 'tis you hide;
> There, none distinguish 'twixt your Shame or Pride,
> Weakness or Delicacy: all so nice,
> That each may seem a Virtue, or a Vice.
>
> (199–206)

Although the public manners of women may be as impene-
trable as those of men, women have so little public
exposure or significance that any resulting obscurity is
trivial at best.

Indeed, just as Pope's lines suggest, all but working-class
women were progressively excluded from participation in
the economy in these early stages in the development of
English capitalism. The increase in large-scale manufacturing
and in the employment of wage labour, and the growing
prosperity of shopkeepers and retailers, combined to make
urban middle-class women consumers rather than
producers. This is the period when wives lose connection

with their husbands' business, when 'spinster' becomes a
term of opprobrium for a useless female dependent rather
than the description of a productive participant in domestic
manufacture and when the leisured lady who takes no
note of business becomes a sign of status and gentility for
well-off tradesmen. Thus, *To a Lady* registers an important
social trend, a trend that — like the Mandevillian public—
private paradox — is clearly a consequence of the new
capitalist mode of production, but in this case an inverted
and gender-specific consequence. *To a Lady*, like *To
Cobham*, ultimately derives its central premises from the
social changes attendant on the early growth of capitalism.
But here the effect of early capitalism's tendency to
devalue women's public role enables Pope to skirt the
paradox of judgement and to assess the characters of
women without contradiction. The unqualified misogyny
of the poem, then, results from its escape from the anxiety
of the failure of judgement, and its vehemence derives at
least in part from the relief and enthusiasm with which it
reinstitutes the categories of knowledge and morality that
seem — at other moments and in other poems — to be
seriously in question. The attack on women frees Pope
from moral ambiguity and formal incoherence; it enables
him to write a strong and uncompromising poem on
human character. In this respect, we could say that Pope
needs to hate women in order to forestall the contradictions associated with the new economic system; his
misogyny has the same source as his 'ethical duet'.

These private women, however, are described in a
strangely public manner. Though they have no actual
public valuation, they are given a public title and function
in a series of metaphors initiated by the famous 'Queen
portrait', the ironic description of Queen Caroline (181—
98) that concludes the tour of female characters in the
poem's portrait gallery. After this, women are repeatedly
'Queens': 'Toasts live a scorn, and Queens may die a jest'
(282), 'Yet mark the fate of a whole Sex of Queens'
(219), 'But ev'ry Lady would be Queen for life' (218).

These last verse paragraphs of the epistle render women almost exclusively through images of power, subjection, tyranny, conquest, retreats, 'foreign glory' and domestic peace (220–43). The irony here works in two ways: to disparage the desire for power in so insignificant and powerless a creature, and, conversely, to create a public identity for a private being. In their direct accessibility to moral judgement, these private women represent Pope's closest approximation to a public male world in which the knowledge and definition of character is secure and unshakeable. In other words, the women in *To a Lady* serve to shore up the notion of a stable, morally determinate identity for men — the primary obsession of Pope's *Epistles* — by their eminently transparent, clearly despicable characterlessness. A strong judgement against women creates the possibility of a similar judgement in the public world of men. Perhaps this need to use women as surrogates for male stability explains the strange incorporeality of their appearance in the poem's most disturbing passage:

> As Hags hold Sabbaths, less for joy than spight,
> So these their merry, miserable Night;
> Still round and round the Ghosts of Beauty glide,
> And haunt the places where their Honour dy'd.

> (239–42)

The women haunting the last section of *To a Lady* are truly ghosts, the ghosts of men from a lost moral system.

If women stand for men in this poem, then where are the 'real' women to be found? Not in the admirable 'Lady' to whom the epistle is addressed. Martha Blount is either 'a softer Man' (272) or an androgyne, mingling the virtues of both sexes. To form her, Heaven

> Picks from each sex, to make the Fav'rite blest,
> Your love of Pleasure, our desire of Rest,
> Blends, in exception to all gen'ral rules,
> Your Taste of Follies, with our Scorn of Fools,

Reserve with Frankness, Art with Truth ally'd,
Courage with Softness, Modesty with Pride,
Fix'd Principles, with Fancy never new;
Shakes all together, and produces — You.

(273—80)

Indeed, there are no substantial women in *To a Lady*. The various women described in the body of the poem are not 'real' women in the way that Wharton in *To Cobham* is a 'real' man, but either ghosts of men or simply pictures of women from the walls of a portrait gallery. As Carole Fabricant has suggested, this kind of portraiture, like landscape-painting and like the verbal pastoral scene-painting of *Windsor-Forest*, reflects an assertion of mastery, a representation of power and possession by which the painter, as well as the viewer/reader, makes the woman or feminized landscape his own.[9] John Berger describes this process as 'the metaphorical act of appropriation' characteristic of the art of this period, an act that could 'render all that is depicted into the hands of the owner-spectator'.[10] Here we have appropriation in its most absolute form. 'Woman' is purely emblematic in the *Epistle to a Lady*. A painting without a model, a sign without a referent, 'woman' holds a place for male fantasy to fill. In *The Rape of the Lock* Belinda creates her identity through her dressing — her connection with the commodities of trade. The representation of 'woman' in *To a Lady* can be seen as the next step in that process of fetishization. Belinda seems to become the products with which she decks herself. The 'characters of women' in *To a Lady* become not products but the reified embodiment of an assertion of moral stability: they stand for a fantasy of unproblematic knowledge and uncontingent judgement, and in that sense they are the most complexly mystified of Pope's poetic creations, pointing toward the historical forces that distort and undermine the philosophical system of the *opus magnum*.

III

Near the conclusion of Epistle III, *To Bathurst* (1733), the speaker asks a 'knotty' (337) question:

> Say, for such worth are other worlds prepared?
> Or are they both, in this their own reward?
>
> (335—6)

He refers most immediately to those who pursue the vice of avarice, and the answer is provided by the career of Sir Balaam, who accumulates riches through a combination of luck, plunder and thievery, rises to a position of wealth and power, and then receives a rapid and concrete earthly punishment:

> My lady falls to play; so bad her chance,
> He must repair it; takes a bribe from France;
> The House impeach him; Coningsby harangues;
> The Court forsake him, and Sir Balaam hangs:
> Wife, son, and daughter, Satan, are thy own,
> His wealth, yet dearer, forfeit to the Crown:
> The Devil and the King divide the prize,
> And sad Sir Balaam curses God and dies.
>
> (395—402)

The poem ends on this note. But several lines earlier the parallel story of the fate of profusion has an outcome whose affect is very different from the approving narration of Sir Balaam's just deserts. Young Cotta, who 'mistook reverse of wrong for right' (200) and, to counter the avarice of his father, spent his fortune, selling his timber, his wool and his lands, which go to equip the English navy and further the imperial cause, finally faces bankruptcy:

> And shall not Britain now reward his toils,
> Britain, that pays her Patriots with her Spoils?
> In vain at Court the Bankrupt pleads his cause,
> His thankless Country leaves him to her Laws.
>
> (215—18)

Young Cotta's punishment is presented rather bitterly as something of an injustice, an ironic reflection upon the nation's gratitude to its patriots, while that of Sir Balaam is unambiguously just, and that of young Cotta's cousin in profligacy from the second half of the poem, 'Great Villiers' (305), is also graphically appropriate. Young Cotta himself, though an emblem of vice, seems at least partially sympathetic. He wasted his estate from 'no mean motive' (205), and his patriotism, as we have seen, is, at least in terms of its benefits to the nation, comparable to Cobham's. Indeed, throughout his poetry Pope cannot represent the suffering of a patriot without some measure of sympathy. The 'knotty' question of the workings of justice is treated in two distinct ways, ways that indicate a familiar incoherence in Pope's philosophical tenets. In fact, *To Bathurst* contains two separate ethical systems, which we can trace through the whole of the poem.

The epistle opens by asserting the premise that the 'use of riches' takes two forms — avarice and profusion:

> Then careful Heav'n supply'd two sorts of Men,
> To squander these, and those to hide agen.
>
> (13—14)

Significantly, these are also Mandeville's key vices, the passions that he sees as most necessary to a successful capitalist economy. Though the society that depends on these passions is treated ironically by Pope, its smooth functioning nevertheless illustrates Heaven's special care for human prosperity. Echoing Epistle II of the *Essay on Man*, Pope describes how the interaction of avarice and profusion ultimately conduces to the public welfare:

> Hear then the truth: ' 'Tis Heav'n each Passion sends,
> 'And diff'rent men directs to diff'rent ends.
> 'Extremes in Nature equal good produce,
> 'Extremes in Man concur to gen'ral use.'
> Ask we what makes one keep, and one bestow?
> That POW'R who bids the Ocean ebb and flow,

Bids seed-time, harvest, equal course maintain,
Thro' reconcil'd extremes of drought and rain,
Builds Life on Death, on Change Duration founds,
And gives th' eternal wheels to know their rounds.

(161—70)

We can find the same argument for the 'gen'ral use' of avarice and profusion in Mandeville: 'I look upon Avarice and Prodigality in the Society as I do upon two contrary Poisons in Physick, of which it is certain that the noxious Qualities being by mutual Mischief corrected in both, they may assist each other, and often make a good Medicine between them.'[11] Mandeville also argues in support of the specifically beneficial economic effects of luxury that we have seen implicit in Pope's ambiguously sympathetic privileging of young Cotta's vice:

> But let us be Just, what Benefit can these things [virtuous moderation] be of, or what earthly Good can they do, to promote the Wealth, the Glory and wordly Greatness of Nations? It is the sensual Courtier that sets no Limits to his Luxury; the Fickle Strumpet that invents new Fashions every Week; the haughty Dutchess that in Equipage, Entertainments, and all her Behavior would imitate a Princess; the profuse Rake and lavish Heir, that scatter about their Money without Wit or Judgment, buy every thing they see, and either destroy or give it away the next Day. . . . It is these that are the Prey and proper Food of a full grown Leviathan; or in other words, such is the calamitous Condition of Human Affairs that we stand in need of the Plagues and Monsters I named to have all the Variety of Labour perform'd, which the Skill of Men is capable of inventing in order to procure an honest Livelihood to the vast Multitudes of working poor, that are required to make a large Society.[12]

The context for Pope's account of 'That POW'R who bids the Ocean ebb and flow' in this epistle is the financial revolution. To Bathurst is about city wealth, paper credit

and South Sea year (119). The first literary account of a
stock-market crash, it describes the South Sea Bubble,
when the boom in inflated South Sea Company stocks
collapsed, many investors were ruined and a few corrupt
company officials made fortunes.[13] The poem is peopled
with the major figures of the world of finance: John
Blunt, a director of the South Sea Company; Gilbert
Heathcote, one of the founders of the Bank of England;
John Ward, a member of Parliament implicated in the
South Sea scheme; and Joseph Gage, a famous stock
speculator.[14] Pope even praises paper credit for its
efficiency in comparison with the clumsy and ridiculous
exchanges of oxen, coals or hogs:

> Blest paper-credit! last and best supply!
> That lends Corruption lighter wings to fly!
> Gold imp'd by thee, can compass hardest things,
> Can pocket States, can fetch or carry Kings;
> A single leaf shall waft an Army o'er,
> Or ship off Senates to a distant Shore;
> A leaf, like Sibyl's, scatter to and fro
> Our fates and fortunes, as the winds shall blow:
> Pregnant with thousands flits the Scrap unseen,
> And silent sells a King or buys a Queen.
>
> (69–78)

Though this passage is clearly ironic, and though Pope's
treatment of the heroes of finance characterizes them as
figures of vice, the epistle's philosophy of concurring
extremes accepts and even celebrates the system that the
poem locally satirizes. The natural and biblical imagery of
'ebbing' and 'flowing', 'seed-time' and 'harvest', 'keeping'
and 'bestowing', refers, at least in the context of this
poem, to the 'natural' financial cycles by which 'blest
paper-credit' maintains economic balance and prosperity.[15]
The analogy is essential to the structure of the poem, but
at the same time it is elusive, hidden, never explicitly
admitted, as if the source of economic and financial order
could be affirmed without ever being acknowledged. From

this perspective the satiric encomium to paper credit is a real tribute that cannot admit its seriousness, and the account of John Blunt's financial manipulations during South Sea year is both sympathetic and ironic: 'Much injur'd Blunt! why bears he Britain's hate?' (135). Howard Erskine-Hill's account of Pope's treatment of Blunt finds 'ambiguity somewhere in the passage', 'moral involvement' and an indication of Pope's consciousness of Blunt's alliance with many of Pope's own friends.[16] Certainly every surface and explicit aspect of the poem's language attacks the corruptions of modern finance, but the system of order that the epistle constructs leads in another direction.

The Cottas belong to this proto-utilitarian system. Old Cotta is avarice. He hosts no feasts, slights his tenants and turns away 'Benighted wanderers' (195). But in the longer perspective, his avarice serves the vital positive function of a 'reservoir' for the profusion of later generations:

> Who sees pale Mammon pine amidst his store,
> Sees but a backward steward for the Poor;
> This year a Reservoir, to keep and spare,
> The next a Fountain, spouting thro' his Heir,
> In lavish streams to quench a Country's thirst,
> And men and dogs shall drink him 'till they burst.
>
> (173—8)

This positive view of the passions has the same ambiguous irony as the encomium to paper credit. The fountain is an image of life and fertility but at the same time a grotesque extreme, evoking a kind of levelling where men and dogs together 'burst' with excessive consumption. Young Cotta, the fountain, matches his father's avarice with an equivalent profusion. As we saw, his passion serves not simply the general welfare, but the specific cause of imperialist expansion. That is, his profusion directly supports the economic system that defines his vice as a public virtue; we don't even have to wait, like Mandeville, for his luxury eventually to employ the 'working poor'.

Significantly and characteristically, Pope's definition of public benefits is located in the economic role of the rural gentry rather than in the contributions of the urban 'Ministers of Industry' that Mandeville tends more frequently to cite. This preference for the country illustrates Pope's personal connection with the landed upper classes, but it also reflects an accurate estimate of a major *locus* of capitalist transformation, at least in the early eighteenth century. Old landowners were the largest consolidators of new wealth in the period, though new fortunes were accumulated by other sources as well. Mandeville may have been more prescient, in that his theories seem almost to predict the operations of a fully industrialized society, but Pope's focus on the capitalist landlords accurately reflects the great movements of rural 'improvement' that served as the precursors of industrialization. As instruments of this kind of public benefit, neither of the Cottas receives a just reward. Indeed, justice is irrelevant to their role in the poem, just as moral judgement is irrelevant to the proto-utilitarian category of 'gen'ral use' within which their avarice and profusion function.

So when Pope turns a few lines later to the advocacy of the 'golden Mean' (246), he is subscribing to a different system. In this scheme, the Man of Ross is the ideal because of his altruism, his selfless attention to the poor, the aged and the sick, and his unqualified and absolute virtue:

> Who builds a Church to God, and not to Fame,
> Will never mark the marble with his Name:
> Go, search it there, where to be born and die,
> Of rich and poor makes all the history;
> Enough, that Virtue fill'd the space between;
> Prov'd, by the ends of being, to have been.
>
> (285–90)

The Man of Ross stands in the same relation to the Cottas of this poem as the virtuous ideal of Epistle IV of the

Essay on Man stands to the proto-utilitarian argument of Epistle II. In both cases, Pope asserts a norm of traditional virtue in a context that at least partly or conditionally invalidates the category of abstract morality itself. Naturally, under the system of the golden mean and the virtuous ideal, the issue of justice — in this world or the next — is an important one. The parable of Sir Balaam illustrates the significance that Pope attaches, at this point in the epistle, to the distinction between vice and virtue. Like the appearance of Cobham at the end of that poem, the vignette of Sir Balaam helps to reinstate by assertion a security of assessment that the body of the epistle tends to erode.[17]

We have been engaged so far in the task of dividing this poem in half, of seeing in the epistle two separate and ir-reconcilable ethical models: one, the opening private vices/public benefits position, which leads to the assertion of 'gen'ral use' and finally to the examples of the Cottas; the other, the rigoristic moral position that begins with the introduction of the ideal of the golden mean and includes the altruistic career of the Man of Ross and the condign punishment of Sir Balaam. But the poem's position is even more complicated than this. Young Cotta, as we have seen, serves as a metaphorical 'fountain' for the capitalist economic system. The Man of Ross, or John Kyrle, our touchstone of pastoral altruism, is celebrated for his construction of a real fountain and waterworks near the river Wye, providing the town of Ross with its first water supply, as well as a public causeway for the use of foot travellers and a new spire on the town church:[18]

> Who hung with woods yon mountain's sultry brow?
> From the dry rock who bade the waters flow?
> Not to the skies in useless columns tost,
> Or in proud falls magnificently lost,
> But clear and artless, pouring thro' the plain
> Health to the sick, and solace to the swain.
> Whose Cause-way parts the vale with shady rows?

> Whose Seats the weary Traveller repose?
> Who taught that heav'n-directed spire to rise?
> The MAN of ROSS, each lisping babe replies.
>
> (253–62)

These projects, interestingly enough, far from being unique to John Kyrle or to the traditional country-house ideal upon which Pope's portrait of the Man of Ross draws, are typical of a major movement for domestic improvement that arose out of the economic prosperity and cultural optimism of the early decades of the eighteenth century.[19] In fact the image of the fountain and waterworks that recurs in *To Bathurst* is one of the tropes of this ideology of public works. Richard Savage in *Of Public Spirit in Regard to Public Works* (1737) echoes Pope's description:

> What though no Streams, in fruitless Pomp display'd,
> Rise a proud Column, fall a grand Cascade;
> Through nether Pipes, which nobler Use renowns,
> Here ductile Riv'lets visit distant Towns![20]

Aside from land and agricultural improvement schemes, characteristic public projects included inland waterways, turnpikes and churches. Daniel Defoe, the age's most prolific advocate and recorder of such projects, summarizes the situation this way:

> 'tis more than probable, that our Posterity may see the Roads all over *England* restor'd in their Time to such a Perfection, that Travelling and Carriage of Goods will be much more easy both to Man and Horse, than ever it was since the *Romans* lost this Island. . . . as for Trade, it will be encourag'd by it every Way . . . . Another Benefit of these new Measures for repairing the Roads by Turnpikes, is the opening of Drains and Watercourses, and Building Bridges. . . . ['if an Account of *Great Britain* was to be written every Year'] every New View . . . would require a New Description; the Improvements that encrease, the New Buildings erected, the Old Buildings

taken down: New Discoveries in Metals, Mines, Minerals; new Undertakings in Trade; Inventions, Engines, Manufactures, in a Nation, pushing and improving as we are: These Things open new Scenes every Day, and make *England* especially shew a new and differing Face in many Places, on every Occasion of Surveying it.[21]

Almost inadvertently, it seems, Pope makes his main exemplar of traditional rigoristic morality also a representative of the concrete works of capitalist prosperity. The Man of Ross would clearly be out of place in a Mandevillian system — in fact, it is the men like Ross with their high moral aims who ruin the prosperous hive in *The Fable of the Bees*. To the extent that Pope sees prosperity in proto-utilitarian terms, the Man of Ross's altruism is inexplicable and anomalous. To the extent that Pope sees an absolute and secure differentiation of vice and virtue as the basic premise of philosophy, young Cotta's 'fountain' of prosperity must be judged and condemned like Sir Balaam's avarice. In the image of the Man of Ross, these two positions are superimposed: that character combines altruism with the projects of an expanding commercial prosperity.

Again, we can apply Pocock's dichotomy between virtue and passion to the incompatible perspectives that we have noted in this poem. For Pocock, as for Pope, the problem of personal morality is closely tied to the rise of a money economy, to the spread of credit and to the substitution of a contingent, local valuation for a static ethical authority. The effect of this contingency, this new conditionality of the terms of moral assessment, was felt in the period as corruption, a theme to which Pope's late satires repeatedly return. Pocock outlines the constellation of issues that we have been treating here:

Once property was seen to have a symbolic value, expressed in coin or credit, the foundations of personality themselves appeared imaginary or at best consensual: the individual could exist, even in his own sight, only at the fluctuating value imposed upon him by his fellows, and these evaluations, though constant and public, were too irrationally performed to be seen as acts of political decision or virtue. . . . the individual engaged in exchange could discern only particular values — that of the commodity which was his, that of the commodity for which he exchanged it. His activity did not oblige or even permit him to contemplate the universal good as he acted upon it, and he consequently continued to lack classical rationality. . . . Techniques certainly existed — of which Addison [and, we might add, Pope] was a literary master — of elevating his motivation to at least the lower forms of rationality and morality; opinion, prudence, confidence, sympathy, even charity; but behind all this lay the ancient problem of showing how society might operate rationally and beneficially when the individuals composing it were denied full rationality and virtue.

Solutions were of course to be found in seeking to depict society as an economic mechanism, in which the exchange of goods and the division of labor operated to turn universal selfishness to universal benefit. . . . But there was a certain sense in which all this was either beside the point or the admission of a necessary evil.[22]

This summary of the dilemma of the period places in clear conjunction the main points raised by our reading of Pope's *opus magnum*: the uncomfortable superimposition of virtue and self-interest, the incongruous alternation between an attack on capitalism and the acceptance of the amoral rule of public benefit and the anxiety-producing elusiveness of a stable character and identity. The figure of the fountain — at once a grotesque and sentimental emblem of capitalist prosperity — illustrates the poetic subtlety with which *To Bathurst* joins this debate.

IV

Epistle IV, *To Burlington* (1731), is even more explicit than *To Bathurst* in specifying the 'improvements' by which prosperity will be spread to the countryside. In the celebratory conclusion of this poem, Pope's friend Burlington is presented as the ideal capitalist landowner, a more fully developed and ambitious version of the Man of Ross, who will build roads, bridges, dams and canals:

> Bid Harbors open, public Ways extend,
> Bid Temples, worthier of the God, ascend;
> Bid the broad Arch the dang'rous Flood contain,
> The Mole projected break the roaring Main;
> Back to his bounds the subject Sea command,
> And roll obedient Rivers thro' the Land.
>
> (197—202)

He will participate, that is, in the essential work of domestic expansion, opening up the country to communication, travel and trade. These patriotic projects are indistinguishable from a corollary contribution to imperialist expansion. The true 'improve[rs of] the Soil' (177) are those, like young Cotta, whose lands directly support the English navy:

> Whose rising Forests, not for pride or show,
> But future Buildings, future Navies grow:
> Let his plantations stretch from down to down,
> First shade a Country, and then raise a Town.
>
> (187—90)

Here Pope joins imperialism with an allusion to the domestic phenomenon of urbanization — the substantial growth of cities and towns in the eighteenth century — which was spurred by the agricultural improvements and enclosures of the capitalist landowners, and which served as an essential precondition of industrialization. No wonder, then, that Pope's celebration of the peace of domestic prosperity at the end of *To Burlington* is perfectly coincident with his evocation of the *pax Britannica*:

> These Honours, Peace to happy Britain brings,
> These are Imperial Works, and worthy Kings.
>
> (203–4)

Like the imagery of the *Essay on Man*, the 'future Navies' and the imperial peace of this poem recollect the language of *Windsor-Forest*.

To Burlington is not only the most explicitly imperialist work in what we have of Pope's *opus magnum*, however. Like *To Bathurst* this epistle is often cited as an example of Pope's debt to Mandeville's proto-utilitarian ethic.[23] The extended satiric account of the visit to Timon's villa, where false magnificence and real discomfort vie for pre-eminence, ends with a familiar passage on the ultimately beneficial effects of even such a grotesque misuse of riches.

> Yet hence the Poor are cloth'd, the Hungry fed;
> Health to himself, and to his Infants bread
> The Lab'rer bears: What his hard Heart denies,
> His charitable Vanity supplies.
>
> (169–72)

The adversative 'yet' that begins this passage almost over-turns the satire that precedes it. Again we encounter the problem of the coexistence of moral judgment and proto-utilitarian valuation. Burlington is commended for his good works, even though the system of private vices/public benefits would seem to be conducive enough to prosperity in itself. Likewise, Timon is condemned as immoral, and yet he serves the general good as well as any altruist. Indeed better. Pope's note to this passage on the poor and hungry suggests, ironically for his moral argument, that Timon is economically preferable to Burlington: 'The *Moral* of the whole, where PROVIDENCE is justified in giving Wealth to those who squander it in this manner.

A bad Taste employs more hands and diffuses Expence more than a good one' (169n.).

In short, *To Burlington* joins a proto-utilitarian economic ethic with the most exact list of plans for capitalist prosperity that we have yet seen in Pope's works. Combined, these two positions give the epistle a programmatic effect, as if it sought to provide a concrete summary of the constituents of capitalist economic prosperity. But, typically, the two routes to this ideal prosperity are strictly incompatible. Timon's method is unconscious and amoral; he serves the general good despite himself, by acting upon his private vice. Burlington's is built upon a set of traditional moral standards and their conventional literary manifestations, upon the trope of the admirable patron of the country house and the perfect reciprocity between his motives and the good taste everywhere evident in his estate. If we turn to that latter notion, we begin to see how Pope obscures the formal contradiction of *To Burlington* by introducing the notions of balance, order and unity that we have already found to be central to the standard of taste derived from neo-classical aesthetics.

Good taste is defined for us in detail in the first part of the epistle. It is connected above all with utility — 'things of use' like Ross's waterworks — and accordingly it is not 'profuse', 'proud' or 'grand'. It is not a product of mere 'glory' or pure 'expence'. Taste derives from 'Good Sense', a 'gift of Heav'n' that reflects a sensitivity to decency, moderation, pleasing variety and a balance by which parts are made to 'slide into a whole' (23—70). To possess good taste means first to follow nature — that neo-classical 'Nature' which must be so carefully and tactfully 'dressed' like the female emblems of displaced cultural expansion:

> In all, let Nature never be forgot.
> But treat the Goddess like a modest fair,
> Nor over-dress, nor leave her wholly bare;
> Let not each beauty ev'ry where be spy'd,
> Where half the skill is decently to hide.   (50—4)

How does this poem demonstrate the proper dressing of nature, the concrete enactment of its theory of taste? Belinda dresses in the spoils of English mercantilism, the sylvan creatures of *Windsor-Forest* dress in the glowing colours of imperialist fantasy, and true wit in the *Essay on Criticism* dresses in the categories of bourgeois civic order and expansionist foreign policy. In the last epistle of the *opus magnum*, nature is dressed by the ordering power of Burlington's 'Imperial Works', the projects of the patriotic aristocrat at home and abroad — towns, bridges, waterworks, public roads, navies and, above all, the ominous 'Peace' of imperialist ideology.

These patriotic projects take a distinctive poetic form in the 'Bid Harbors' passage that we have already examined, a form very close to that which represents the ordering power of nature in the central verses of *To Bathurst*:

> Ask we what makes one keep, and one bestow?
> That POW'R who bids the Ocean ebb and flow,
> Bids seed-time, harvest, equal course maintain.
>
> (165—7)

In each of these passages the prominent rhetorical effect is balanced antithesis. Burlington's constructions will both 'open' and 'contain', just as the concurring extremes in nature 'keep' and 'bestow'. The *concordia discors* here seems dependent on the image of waters or seas; the lines from *To Burlington* juxtapose and reconcile the 'roaring Main' and the 'subject Sea', the 'dang'rous Flood' and 'obedient Rivers', like *To Bathurst*'s concern with the 'ebb and flow' of the ocean. But more interesting and perhaps less obvious is the strange dual agency embodied in the lines. Both Burlington and his works act: like God at the creation, Burlington 'bids' and his harbors 'open', his public ways 'extend', his temples 'ascend', and his bridges 'contain'; nature 'bids' and the seasons 'maintain' their course. The lines in these passages are typically framed by verbs, one expressing the agency of the ordering power and the other that of the obedient subject in a reciprocal arrangement of perfect control and perfect co-operation where one slides into the other.

We have seen this kind of verbal reciprocity elsewhere. The pastoral good works of the Man of Ross, for instance, illustrate the same structure in an interrogative mode:

> Who hung with woods yon mountain's sultry brow?
> From the dry rock who bade the waters flow?
> . . .
> Whose Cause-way parts the vale with shady rows?
> . . .
> Who taught the heav'n-directed spire to rise?
>
> (253—61)

Again, the spire rises and the waters seem to flow by themselves, autonomously, though under Ross's command. The same simultaneity of control and concession characterizes an earlier passage in *To Burlington* describing the task of the landscape gardener who dresses the female countryside:

> Consult the Genius of the Place in all;
> That tells the Waters or to rise, or fall,
> Or helps th' ambitious Hill the heav'ns to scale,
> Or scoops in circling theatres the Vale,
> Calls in the Country, catches opening glades,
> Joins willing woods, and varies shades from shades,
> Now breaks or now directs, th' intending Lines;
> Paints as you plant, and, as you work, designs.
>
> (57—64)

In fact the agency is tripled here: the passage superimposes the gardener who 'plants' and 'works' upon the 'Genius of the Place', which 'tells' the waters what to do, 'scoops' the valleys, and 'joins' the woods. And both are simultaneously aided by the 'willing' landscape itself, the waters rising, the glades opening, and the hills scaling the heavens to provide a setting of aesthetic perfection. We can even find a version of this rhetoric in the opening pastoral scene of *Windsor-Forest*:

Here in full light the russet Plains extend;
There wraps in Clouds the blueish Hills ascend.
                                              (23—4)

Though there is no opening verb here, like the 'bidding' or 'calling' or 'teaching' of the prior examples, the hills ascend and the plains extend at the implicit command of the poet's ordering vision and with the same rhyming words as *To Burlington*'s extend/ascend couplet (197—8). Both Pope and Burlington shape a willing setting: but where *Windsor-Forest* paints pastoral plains and hills, Burlington builds imperial harbours, roads, temples and moles. In *To Burlington* as in *Windsor-Forest*, there is more to Pope's landscape than meets the eye. Both poems enact a characteristic convergence of the pastoral and the imperial, in which the natural world is 'charmed', transformed, magically made over in the mirror of ideology. When we read the poems together, we can see both versions of each landscape; we can discover the balanced vistas of *Windsor*'s pastoral behind Burlington's imperial projects, and reciprocally, we can glimpse the harbours and moles of rural improvement in the hills and woods of the 'natural' setting of Windsor Forest.

The rhetoric of reciprocal command and concession that marks the concluding 'Bid Harbors' passage of *To Burlington* uncovers a rich complex of related ideological structures: from pastoral and patriotism to misogyny and neo-classical aesthetics. The collaboration that Burlington imposes upon his setting is the prototypical neo-classical act, the 'True Wit' that 'gives us back the Image of our Mind', the ultimate form of expansionist appropriation. Burlington's language of collaboration recalls the 'poor Indian' of the *Essay on Man*, who is made to testify to the inevitability of power and oppression. Here the countryside of England is made to 'extend' and 'ascend' in enthusiastic anticipation of the commands of the imperialist. But this is also an act of the fullest possible patriotism. In pursuing good taste and shaping his landscape as he does, Burlington serves as a figure of public virtue, a source of national prosperity. Likewise, in thus contributing to the economic welfare and peace of the empire, he fulfils an aesthetic ideal. The structure of command and concession embodied in that ideal reproduces the process of appropriation by which the goddess of the natural scene is dressed to advantage, possessed, mastered and maintained. The image of the woman lies hidden behind the pastoral landscape, the rhetoric of collaboration and the neo-classical trope of the 'dressing' of nature by true wit. In this sense the private figure of the woman can be said to stand for the whole constellation of ideological structures that the poem elaborates.[24]

To Burlington is an appropriate summary statement for the *opus magnum*, a compendium of the ideological constituents of Pope's major poetry. Its aim is the formation of an ideology which we have come to call 'Augustan humanism' — the definition of a cultural ideal for the ruling class, an ideal constructed from the superimposition of an abstract and neo-classical system of aesthetic valuation upon a concrete programme for mercantile capitalist economic expansion.[25] It is this superimposition that provides the poem with a thematic coherence — in the notion of taste — to weigh against the evaluative incoherence between Timon's vice and Burlington's virtue. Though both are efficacious in the new economy, that contradiction is obscured in the unifying concern with taste. But taste means even more to the poem than a nominal formal unity. Burlington's tasteful projects have been described as the epitome of Pope's vision of 'Augustan humanism'.[26] This reading substantiates that claim, but it also calls such a humanism into question. My questions are not new ones, however. They were already being asked, in a different manner, by the poets of the mid-eighteenth century. Burlington's 'Imperial Works' are predominantly waterworks: harbours, bridges to contain the 'dang'rous

'Flood', the 'Mole' to command the ocean and the 'obedient Rivers' carrying commerce 'thro' the Land'. We have seen these waters before: in the Thames that runs 'strong without rage' in Denham's famous couplet; in the seas that bear the forests of the English navy to the New World in *Windsor-Forest*, and in the fountain and the reservoir that guarantee economic prosperity in *To Bathurst* — in short, throughout the major imagery of mercantile expansion. These are the prototypical waters of the neo-classical *concordia discors*. But they flow with a different effect in another major poem of the period, a poem written almost a half-century after Pope's:

> And thou, sweet Poetry, . . .
> . . . with thy persuasive strain
> Teach erring man to spurn the rage of gain;
> Teach him that states of native strength possessed,
> Though very poor, may still be very blest;
> That trade's proud empire hastes to swift decay,
> As ocean sweeps the labour'd mole away.[27]

The graphic overturning of the mole, which is swept away in Goldsmith's and Johnson's lines by the very seas that it commanded in Pope's poem, marks the ideological shift in literature and especially poetry that accompanies the close of England's first imperial period in the second half of the eighteenth century. The formal failure and obsolescence of the *concordia discors*, the attitude of lament and loss, and the images of destruction and decay that replace Pope's hopeful landscapes of extension and ascension, all indicate a repudiation of imperialist apologia. *The Deserted Village*, with its indictment of the social costs of mercantile expansion, commercial prosperity and the transformation of English culture by urbanization, enclosure and agricultural modernization, anticipates the romantic critique of industrialization, and it grounds that critique in one of Pope's strongest images of imperial power.

V

At this point in our discussion of the four *Epistles to Several Persons*, the question of why Pope's *opus magnum* could not be written may seem a little less 'knotty'. We have confronted, after all, a series of incoherent or contradictory poems, embodying all the extremes of inconsistency, mystification and appropriation in Pope's commodious repertory. Indeed the problem could perhaps more effectively be restated as the question of why Pope wrote as much of the *opus magnum* as he did, why he persisted beyond the *Essay on Man* in rephrasing the contradictions that he obviously could not escape or resolve. *To Burlington* gives us our best answer to this question. Pope's advocacy of rural 'improvements' in that poem is sometimes taken as anomalous, inconsistent with the political disillusionment of this period in his career.[28] In our reading of Pope's corpus, however, these 'Imperial Works' are a sign of his continued allegiance to the new mode of production despite his specific quarrels with its implementation, a benchmark of his formal and ideological implication in capitalism. The *opus magnum* could not be written because it takes this implication as a problem to be resolved. As we have seen in our reading of the *Epistles* and the *Essay on Man*, Pope's problem engages a major historical transition in a way that allows for no resolution. The formal incoherence, the imagistic ambivalence and the ideological complexity that we have uncovered in these poems demonstrate the extent to which they live out the paradoxes of their historical moment. But in fact the very failure of this poetry to move beyond its time is also its enabling 'advantage', the constraint that assures its significance. The futility of Pope's struggle to assert a non-contingent and absolute standard of judgement generates that famous adversary stance of his late poetry, the stance of the virtuous satirist, the privileged arbiter whose vehement defiance takes on history itself:

Ask you what Provocation I have had?
The strong Antipathy of Good to Bad.
When Truth or Virtue an Affront endures,
Th'Affront is mine, my Friend, and should be yours.
. . .
Mine, as a Friend to ev'ry worthy mind;
And mine as Man, who feel for all mankind.

(*Epilogue to the Satires* [1738],
Dialogue II, 197—204)

Pope's own 'True Wit', then, derives its 'advantage' from the contradictions and contingencies of its context, much as Belinda makes her beauty from the materials of a commodified culture.

4 The New Pastoral –
Capitalism and Apocalypse:
The Dunciad (1728, 1742, 1743)

The Dunciad can be seen as an extended summary of
Pope's poetic career. Chronologically, its composition and
publication stretches across the whole of his second major
phase of original production. Pope describes his plans for
an 'investigation of my own Territories. ... something
domestic, fit for my own country, and for my own time'.[1]
in a letter to Swift shortly after the publication of his
edition of Shakespeare in 1725, and he seems to have
begun writing an early draft of the poem even before his
Odyssey was out of his hands in 1726.[2] The first version,
in three books with Lewis Theobald as hero, was published
in 1728. The second version, *The Dunciad Variorum*,
including extensive annotations and textual apparatus,
came out during the following year. And in 1742, after the
decade of the 1730s, which saw the publication of the
Essay on Man, the *Epistles to Several Persons* and the
Imitations of Horace, Book IV was published separately as
The New Dunciad with Colley Cibber as its hero. Finally,
in 1743, only a few months before his death, Pope
published the whole revised poem in four books with
Colley Cibber installed as protagonist throughout, in the
last substantial act of his literary career.

Poetically, as well, *The Dunciad* seems to summarize a
corpus. It is a selective compendium of Pope's earlier

works, particularly the *Messiah*, *The Temple of Fame*, *The Rape of the Lock*, the *Essay on Man* and *Windsor-Forest*. And it brings to an unexpected culmination a variety of the images and formal tropes upon which Pope predicated his major poetry: pastoral scene-painting, *concordia discors*, catalogue rhetoric, and the powerful and complex image of the new world. Ideologically, too, *The Dunciad* comprehends the problematic position of Pope's poetry, shedding a special light on the early work and on the corpus as a whole. In its reactionary rendering of apocalypse, *The Dunciad* teaches us the most radical reading of Pope's poetry; paradoxically, we can see — in this poem's insistence on the end of history — its embodiment of historical process, as well as the historical significance of the earlier works it repeats and rewrites. We must therefore read *The Dunciad* back and forth across Pope's corpus — in *The Rape of the Lock*, the *Essay on Man* and especially *Windsor-Forest* — as well as in itself.

I

Like *The Rape of the Lock*, *The Dunciad* deals in commodities. The first of its catalogues of exchangeable goods stands near the beginning of Book I, in the description of the journals and magazines — the least respectable products of an expanding printing industry — produced in Dulness's cave and released from there upon the world:

> Hence Miscellanies spring, the weekly boast
> Of Curl's chaste press, and Lintot's rubric post:
> Hence hymning Tyburn's elegiac lines,
> Hence Journals, Medleys, Merc'ries, Magazines:
> Sepulchral Lyes, our holy walls to grace,
> And New-year Odes, and all the Grub-street race.
>
> ([B] I, 39–44)

These are all literary commodities, collected here as a concrete emblem of the crass materialism of booksellers and hack writers and the capitalization of literary culture. This passage gives the same impression of random enumeration as the first commodity catalogue that we identified in Pope's poetry: the list of spoils on Belinda's dressing table. And the single compressed line of alliterative objects — 'Hence Journals, Medleys, Merc'ries, Magazines' — reproduces the cumulative rhythm of 'Puffs, Powders, Patches, Bibles, Billet-doux'. Indeed the alliteration itself, here and elsewhere in Pope's lists, contributes to the effect of indiscriminate accumulation by projecting the possibility of an infinity of like-sounding words, as if any noun beginning in 'm' and ending in 's' could be substituted with identical euphony. In this passage, that euphony leads to direct attack, to a satire much less ambivalent than that of *The Rape of the Lock*. Our examination of the language — or the various languages — of commodity fetishism in *The Dunciad* will enable us to find an ideological location for this difference of tone.

The attack on the capitalization of the printing industry and hence of literature itself is the main explicit enterprise of *The Dunciad*. Pope's role is that of the adversary of modern publishers and booksellers who weigh 'truth with gold' and pursue only material reward — 'solid pudding' rather than 'empty praise' ([B] I, 53–4). The poem is populated by contemporary Grub Street figures, who outdo each other in crassness and depravity. And yet, as one of Pope's bibliographers exclaims, 'If Pope is not the greatest among English poets, he is the greatest advertiser and publisher among them.'[3] During a period when writers were often at the mercy of booksellers' monopolies, Pope understood the industry better than his publishers, regularly besting them in commercial and contractual arrangements.[4] He acquired a substantial financial independence very early in his career with the *Iliad* subscription, which is said to have earned him £5,320.[5] These subscriptions were profitable ventures in which subscribers paid in advance of publication for an elegantly appointed book, and also in part for the prestige of being listed among the cultured supporters of Pope's work. But although the subscriptions — the *Iliad*, the *Odyssey*, and the Shakespeare edition — were supported by the aristocracy, even that apparent vestige of patronage is deceptive. His subscribers were not consistently eager to offer their support, nor did they represent a homogeneous and stable group of patrons upon whom the poet could rely. In fact, Pope's commercial manipulations — his advertisements, promotional arrangements and contractual negotiations with his publisher Bernard Lintot — were crucial factors in the success of his subscriptions. As Pat Rogers has shown, 'Pope's "triumph" was largely financial rather than social.'[6] Pope was also a commercial innovator on his own behalf. Later in his career he was able, in part, to circumvent the monopolistic power of the publishers by working directly with his own printer and selling his printed works himself to the book-sellers. And at the end of his life, ever sensitive to trends in the market, he changed his publishing format to respond to new demands for cheaper, smaller-scale editions that would be affordable by a larger number of readers. His explanation of this decision decisively contradicts his life-long claim that he cared nothing for profits, but only for virtue and truth; he values his works in terms of their worth in the marketplace: 'I have done with expensive Editions for ever, which are only a Complement to a few curious people at the expence of the Publisher, & to the displeasure of the Many. . . . for the time to come, the World shall not pay, nor make Me pay, more for my Works than they are worth.'[7] Pope's relation to the printing industry is a problematic and ambivalent one. The representation of the capitalization of literature in *The Dunciad* has a parallel ambivalence, a shifting significance that we can begin to see registered in the rhetoric of commodity fetishism.

The Rape of the Lock and *Windsor-Forest* introduce the language of commodity fetishism in a few isolated and relatively brief passages. Though other formal features of both poems, especially the use of zeugma in *The Rape of the Lock* and pastoral scene-painting in *Windsor-Forest*, produce poetic effects similar to that created by catalogue rhetoric, listing language is not in itself constitutive of either work. In *The Dunciad*, by contrast, lists appear everywhere. Irvin Ehrenpreis has argued that the poem is made up of a collection of detached catalogues, files, sequences of names, 'lists of specimens' and 'parade[s] of apparently similar items'.[8] In the following passage, for instance, the list takes the form of a series of prepositional phrases describing the dress, place of origin and mode of transportation of the contestants summoned to the epic games of Book II:

> And now the Queen, to glad her sons, proclaims
> By herald Hawkers, high heroic Games.
> They summon all her Race: an endless band
> Pours forth, and leaves unpeopled half the land.
> A motley mixture! in long wigs, in bags,
> In silks, in crapes, in Garters, and in rags,
> From drawing rooms, from colleges, from garrets,
> On horse, on foot, in hacks, and gilded chariots:
> All who true Dunces in her cause appear'd,
> And all who knew those Dunces to reward.
>
> ([B] II, 17—26)

'Motley mixture' is the key phrase here: it describes the effect of randomness, illogic and raw accumulation that we found in the imperialist catalogues of Pope's earlier works. And the same tension reigns between phonetic congruence and the indiscriminacy of items: 'wigs', 'bags' and 'rags' are all linked in sound and syllable, though the wearing of 'long wigs' designates the opposite of 'rags' in the social world. The flocking of the dunces to Dulness's games is rhetorically identical to the flowing of magazines and journals from Dulness's cave. In both cases the primary poetic effect is pure numerousness, an inexhaustible and indistinguishable accumulation. But here human figures — or at least their accoutrements — take the place of commodities.

Pope exploits the failure of discrimination endemic to these lists in a variety of ways. Sometimes the catalogue leads toward deflation:

> Hence the Fool's Paradise, the Statesman's Scheme,
> The air-built Castle, and the golden Dream,
> The Maid's romantic wish, the Chemist's flame,
> And Poet's vision of eternal Fame.
>
> ([B] III, 9—12)

The effect of this pair of couplets is like that produced in a single line in the prototypical 'Puffs, Powders, Patches, Bibles, Billet-doux'. The last unit, in both passages, is the longest: 'Billet-doux' and 'poet's vision of eternal fame'. In both cases it serves as a phonetic climax, which would seem therefore to make it unique, separate in some way from the other items in the list. But instead its effect is reductive, its distinctiveness turns into congruence; the poet, despite our hopes or assumptions, is no different from the romantic maid or the fool. The pervasive catalogues of *The Dunciad* allow no distinctions: the poem is constituted by lists, and it seems to list and level everything.

The inclusion of 'Bibles' in the items of Belinda's toilet illustrates the kind of ironic incongruity that Pope's commodity catalogues can exploit, but it only give us a partial model for the diverse listing rhetoric typical of *The Dunciad*. 'Bibles' are surprising because they are not usually classified with 'Powders' and 'Billet-doux'. Still, we can visualize a Bible among those items on Belinda's dressing table, as well as a society where Bibles might be used for the same ends as powders and patches. The issue of incongruity becomes increasingly complicated in *The Dunciad*. This couplet from the *Imitations of Horace* can serve as an intermediate example, a means of transition from the simple commodity catalogue to the more elaborate and difficult lists of *The Dunciad*:

> Pageants on pageants, in long order drawn,
> Peers, Heralds, Bishops, Ermin, Gold, and Lawn.
>
> (Ep. II.i, 316—17)

'Ermin, Gold, and Lawn' would be visible in a pageant of 'Peers, Heralds, [and] Bishops', but this line places the materials of which their clóthes are made in the same category as the individuals themselves, or the offices those individuals occupy. The deflation here is the movement toward the material, a movement typical of commodity fetishism, and one which we have already observed in the 'wigs and bags' description of the dunces in Book II. In fact, this passage concisely exhibits the move by which the commodity list is extended to include potentially anything. The second line is divided exactly in half between material products — stuff like that of the trade catalogues we examined in conjunction with *The Rape of the Lock*, '*Indigo, Muslins, Cotton-yarn*' — and human beings or categories of social status. If we leave off the dry goods, we are left with a commodity catalogue that lists not commodities, but people or concepts as commodities. This transformation of the 'objects' of the catalogue beyond the material is a grotesque fulfilment of commodity fetishism that Lukács, extrapolating from Marx, called reification. Not only are social relations between people seen as relations between things, but all aspects of human experience, including institutions and intellectual paradigms, take on the reductively objectified and standardized features of the commodity.[9]

The juxtaposition of 'Bibles' and 'Powders' or 'Bishops' and 'Lawn' tests the capacities of the catalogue by forcing unusual or ironic congruities into the euphonious couplet. This kind of testing becomes more strenuous when the terms being compared do not even inhabit the same universe of discourse. In the noise contest of Book II:

> Now thousand tongues are heard in one loud din:
> The Monkey-mimics rush discordant in;
> 'Twas chatt'ring, grinning, mouthing, jabb'ring all,
> And Noise and Norton, Brangling and Breval,
> Dennis and Dissonance, and captious Art,
> And Snip-shap short, and Interruption smart,

And Demonstration thin, and Theses thick,
And Major, Minor, and Conclusion quick.
                                    ([B] II, 235–42)

This passage takes indiscriminate accumulation to its
logical extreme, levelling the names of real writers —
Benjamin Norton Defoe, John Durant Breval and John
Dennis — with sounds and descriptions of audible disputa-
tion — 'Noise', 'Brangling' and 'Dissonance' — and, in a
rush of disruptive inventiveness, with terms from logical
argumentation — 'Demonstration' and 'Theses' — and the
structure of the syllogism — 'Major', 'Minor' and 'Conclusion'. The radical incompatibility of the items seems to
entail an equivalently extreme euphony in the line: 'Noise
and Norton', 'Brangling and Breval', and 'Dennis and
Dissonance' have more than the usual phonetic resem-
blances. Assonance and additional alliteration bring these
pairs closer even than our prototypical 'Puffs, Powders'.
This passage, then, moves in two opposite directions. On
the one hand, it advertises with an exceptional inventiveness the heroic couplet's capacity to join disparate or incoherent forces into an ordered totality. On the other
hand, it stretches the movement of commodification that
we have been tracing in the 'journals and magazines' and
the 'wigs and bags' passages to the point of full fragmenta-
tion. When proper nouns, noises and abstract qualities are
listed as if they were objects, nothing can retain its
autonomy, and here not only the persons of the dunces
but human action and discourse itself are reified.

   A parallel passage shows the extension of this process of
reification to literature:

   Here to her Chosen all her works she shews;
   Prose swell'd to verse, verse loit'ring into prose:
   How random thoughts now meaning chance to find,
   Now leave all memory of sense behind:
   How Prologues into Prefaces decay,
   And these to Notes are fritter'd quite away:
   How Index-learning turns no student pale,

Yet holds the eel of science by the tail:
How, with less reading than makes felons scape,
Less human genius than God gives an ape,
Small thanks to France, and none to Rome or Greece,
A past, vamp'd, future, old, reviv'd, new piece,
'Twixt Plautus, Fletcher, Shakespeare, and Corneille,
Can make a Cibber, Tibbald, or Ozell.

([B] I, 273–86)

The 'motly mixture' of Dulness's literary works — represented through an accumulation of adjectives and proper
names — despite its specificity, produces an effect of
indeterminacy in which no single literary product or mode
— 'prose', 'verse', 'Prologue' or 'Notes' — can remain fixed
and defined. The three lists in the last three lines of the
passage enact this arbitrariness in their juxtaposition of
contradictory terms — 'old' and 'new', 'past' and 'future' —
as well as of qualities and proper names. And yet the
farther the items move from similarity and coherence in
the commodity catalogue, the greater the effort of the
couplet to join them together.

In Book III, the vision of Dulness's kingdom to come is
introduced with the same kind of listing rhetoric:

All sudden, Gorgons hiss, and Dragons glare,
And ten-horn'd fiends and Giants rush to war.
Hell rises, Heav'n descends, and dance on Earth:
Gods, imps, and monsters, music, rage, and mirth,
A fire, a jigg, a battle, and a ball,
'Till one wide conflagration swallows all.

([B] III, 235–40)

This catalogue has passed beyond Norton and Dennis or
Cibber and Shakespeare, beyond the names of the dunces
or the texts they produce, to a fantasy of unrestricted
indiscriminacy. We would not know, without the prior
examples as a formal ground, the connection of this scene
with the rhetoric of commodification. In fact, it follows all
the formal rules that we defined in the 'journals and

magazines' or the 'Puffs, Powders' inventories. The alliterative connection of 'monsters' and 'music' or 'battle' and 'ball' phonetically joins incongruous items and calls up all the forces of proliferation that we have identified in the commodity catalogue. As Pope's lists move further from the concrete commodities with which we began our analysis, and as more disparate and disjunctive terms enter the realm of reification, the verse becomes progressively more excessive and fantastic, its differences more extreme and its conjunctions more extraordinary. This increasingly disruptive energy is set loose here. The rhythm of the passage suggests a growing intensity — from the multi-syllabic 'ten-horn'd fiends and Giants' through the tri-syllabic near-dactyls of 'Hell rises, Heav'n descends . . . dance on Earth' to the linked monosyllables 'A fire, a jigg, a battle, and a ball'. And the list's momentum gives birth to 'a new world to Nature's laws unknown' ([B] III, 241). The language of commodity fetishism itself generates *The Dunciad*'s apocalypse, just as, in *Windsor-Forest*, the lists of imperial products lead to the 'naturally' forthcoming millennium of the *pax Britannica*.

The rhetoric of commodification, then, with its extension into reification, provides a form for the representation of the cultural effects of capitalism — a form whose use stretches from the beginning of Pope's career to the end. In this sense, it links *The Dunciad* with *Windsor-Forest* and *The Rape of the Lock*, supplying one specific piece of evidence for a coherence in Pope's corpus. But the consistency I am constructing here must also be seen in terms of difference. In *Windsor-Forest* cataloguing rhetoric is the poetic embodiment of imperialism, of a fascination with the accumulation of the products of trade. The products themselves and their sublimation into sylvan creatures are alluring in their evocation or riches — gold, silver and precious gems — and seductive in their visual appeal. Though we have seen their close connection with the violence of imperial power — the 'bleeding' of the pheasant and the balm — their primary immediate effect is captivating, entrancing, beautiful. The 'spoils' of Belinda's toilet are similarly attractive and desirable. Only the moral anarchy of 'Puffs, Powders, Patches, Bibles, Billet-doux' casts doubt on the positive pleasures of accumulation.

In *The Dunciad*, however, listing language refers not to imperial imports but to the domestic products of capitalism. These products are neither colourful nor alluring, as they are in *Windsor-Forest* and *The Rape of the Lock*. They are weird, grotesque, fantastic and hyperactive. The valence and dimensions of the representation of obsessive accumulation have shifted with the transference of its ground from imperialism to capitalism, the generative force behind foreign expansion. Yet in all these poems commodification becomes inclusive. That is, the extension of the list from magazines and journals to the dunces themselves and to logic, literature and art in general is *The Dunciad*'s equivalent of *Windsor-Forest*'s translation of imperial products into the pastoral pheasant and fish, and of *The Rape of the Lock*'s commodification of Belinda herself as she becomes the spoils with which she is dressed. In *The Dunciad* this movement of reification is bolder, more extensive, and more explicitly disturbing than in *Windsor-Forest* or *The Rape of the Lock*, just as the description of the listed products themselves is less apparently appealing.

Even though *The Dunciad*'s treatment of capitalism diverges substantially from *Windsor-Forest*'s and *The Rape of the Lock*'s treatments of imperialism, the juxtaposition of the language of commodity fetishism in these three works gives us a perspective on each of them unavailable without this formal common denominator. It enables us to perceive the flat indiscriminacy of the imperialist catalogues, despite their gaudy colours, and to discover their fetishizing, dehumanizing or — in the case of *Windsor-Forest*'s pastoral creatures — de-animating implications. And it permits us to see the fascinating and generative dimension of *The Dunciad*'s reified collections of names, noises and magazines. In other words, if we take Pope's catalogue rhetoric as the sign of a complex, multiply displaced and intricately layered ideological construct, then we can use it as a formal lever against the various mystifications of Pope's individual works, reading one against another — the apology for imperialism against the invective upon the printing industry — to produce an insight beyond the capacity of any single poem: the insight of the form itself in ideological practice.

II

The pastoral material that we last glimpsed in the balanced vistas of Burlington's 'Imperial Works' plays a significant part in *The Dunciad*'s apocalyptic scene-painting. The new landscape of Dulness's kingdom is introduced near the opening of Book I, shortly after the account of the flood of magazines and journals from Dulness's cave. The crucial pastoral moment is prefaced by a description of the chaos of language and literature in Dulness's empire, specifically the unnatural violations of the neo-classical conventions of genre and verisimilitude — the unities of time and place — in the drama:

> She sees a Mob of Metaphors advance,
> Pleas'd with the madness of the mazy dance:
> How Tragedy and Comedy embrace;
> How Farce and Epic get a jumbled race;
> How Time himself stands still at her command,
> Realms shift their place, and Ocean turns to land.
> Here gay description Ægypt glads with show'rs,
> Or gives to Zembla fruits, to Barca flow'rs;
> Glitt'ring with ice here hoary hills are seen,
> There painted vallies of eternal green,
> In cold December fragrant chaplets blow,
> And heavy harvests nod beneath the snow.
>
> ([B] I, 67—78)

These lines, as Pope's note indicates, are meant to 'represent the inconsistencies in the description of Poets, who heap together all glittering and gawdy Images, tho' incompatible in one season, or in one scene'.[10] Pope condems this device elsewhere. In his *Guardian* essay of 1713 'On the Subject of Pastorals', reprinted as an appendix to *The Dunciad Variorum*, Pope satirizes Ambrose Philips for a similar incongruity: 'Mr. *Philips*, by a poetical Creation, hath raised up finer beds of Flowers than the most industrious Gardiner; his Roses, Endives, Lillies, Kingcups and Daffodils blow *all in the same season.*'[11] And in *Peri Bathous* Pope indicts the same climatic incongruity in his satiric condemnation of:

> The MIXTURE of FIGURES, which raises so many Images, as to give you no Image at all. But its principal Beauty is when it gives an Idea just opposite to what it seem'd meant to describe. Thus an ingenious Artist painting the *Spring*, talks of a *Snow* of *Blossoms*, and thereby raises an unexpected Picture of *Winter*.[12]

Clearly the oxymoronic images of this scene from *The Dunciad* — harvests and snow, December and 'fragrant chaplets', 'hoary hills' and green valleys — are intended as an attack upon the violations of natural order perpetrated in literature by the dunces. But if we read these lines against the prior use of pastoral convention in Pope's corpus, we can supply them with a series of precedents that makes them seem much less perverse than *The Dunciad* seems to warrant. They recall the climactic passage of the *Messiah* (1712), which records the earth's celebration of the coming of the saviour:

> The Swain in barren Desarts with/surprize [shall]
> See Lillies spring, and sudden verdure rise;
> And Starts, amidst the thirsty Wilds, to hear
> New Falls of Water murm'ring in his Ear:
> On rifted Rocks, the Dragon's late Abodes,
> The green Reed trembles, and the Bulrush nods.

Waste sandy Vallies, once perplex'd with Thorn,
The spiry Firr and shapely Box adorn;
To leaf-less Shrubs the flow'ring Palms succeed,
And od'rous Myrtle to the noisome Weed.

(67—76)

Admittedly, these marvels have a special licence from the Nativity; verisimilitude holds less authority over Christian miracles. But we can draw the same parallel with our prototypical pastoral moment from *Windsor-Forest*:

Here waving Groves a chequer'd Scene display,
And part admit and part exclude the Day;
. . .
There, interspers'd in Lawns and opening Glades,
Thin Trees arise that shun each others Shades.
Here in full Light the russet Plains extend;
There wrapt in Clouds the blueish Hills ascend:
Ev'n the wild Heath displays her purple Dies,
And 'midst the Desert fruitful Fields arise,
That crown'd with tufted Trees and springing Corn,
Like verdant Isles the sable Waste adorn.

(17—28)

This is a piece of earthly, post-lapsarian, pre-millennial scene-painting whose oxymorons, as we saw in our reading of the tensions of *Windsor-Forest*, cannot be rationalized away. These passages all obviously portray a similar scene — the image of a 'sudden Verdure', a miraculous and surprising fertility — based on contrast and unlikely juxtaposition and presented in the characteristic structures of Pope's pastoral language, where the poet and viewer join their actions with nature's, and the 'harvest nods', the 'Reed trembles', the 'Verdure rise[s]' and the 'Hills ascend' at their bidding. If *The Dunciad*'s pastoral scene is grotesque, ridiculous or aesthetically pernicious, as Pope's comments would have it, then these parallel moments in *Windsor-Forest* and the *Messiah* must be at least partially problematic as well. And if the latter passages are celebratory and generative, we must find something of that celebration and generation in *The Dunciad*.

Again, at the dramatic description of the coming of the kingdom of Dulness in the vision that concludes Book III, *The Dunciad* gives us a disturbing inversion of pastoral, based, as Pope tells us, on some of the more spectacular effects of the contemporary theatre:

> Thence a new world to Nature's laws unknown,
> Breaks our refulgent, with a heav'n its own:
> Another Cynthia her new journey runs,
> And other planets circle other suns.
> The forests dance, the rivers upward rise,
> Whales sport in woods, and dolphins in the skies;
> And last, to give the whole creation Grace,
> Lo! one vast Egg produces human race.
>
> ([B] III, 241–8)

And again, we can compare a series of significant precedents. In *The Temple of Fame* (1715), Pope's early Chaucerian imitation:

> Here *Orpheus* sings; Trees moving to the Sound
> Start from their Roots, and form a Shade around:
> *Amphion* there the loud creating Lyre
> Strikes, and behold a sudden Thebes aspire!
> *Cythæron*'s Echoes answer to his Call,
> And half the Mountain rolls into a Wall:
> There might you see the length'ning Spires ascend,
> The Domes swell up, the widening Arches bend,
> The growing Tow'rs like Exhalations rise,
> And the huge Columns heave into the Skies.
>
> (83–92)

In the second pastoral, *Summer* (1709):

> The wondring Forests soon shou'd dance again,
> The moving Mountains hear the pow'rful Call,
> And headlong Streams hang list'ning in their Fall!
>
> (82–4)

In the *Messiah*:

> See lofty *Lebanon* his Head advance,
> See nodding Forests on the Mountain dance.
>
> (25—6)

And in a now-familiar passage from *Windsor-Forest*:

> Oft in her glass the musing Shepherd spies
> The headlong Mountains and the downward Skies,
> The watry Landskip of the pendant Woods,
> And absent Trees that tremble in the Floods;
> In the clear azure Gleam the Flocks are seen,
> And floating Forests paint the Waves with Green.
>
> (211—16)

The skies are 'downward' here, while in *The Dunciad* the rivers rise 'upward', and the trees are merely trembling, while in *The Dunciad*, as in the *Messiah* and *Summer*, they dance in a kind of enthusiastic extension of the movement weakly indicated in *Windsor-Forest*. The comparison of these scenes reveals an increased activity in *The Dunciad* as compared to *Windsor-Forest*; *The Dunciad* serves to open up *Windsor-Forest*'s pastoral imagery, to release the energies that the earlier poem keeps largely hidden and rationalized, almost as if *The Dunciad* were the original version, and *Windsor-Forest*'s pastorals the once-removed reductions from a potent source.

In fact these scenes figure in exactly this way in their relation to one of their main common sources, the description of the creation in Book VII of *Paradise Lost*:

> . . . God said, Let there be firmament
> Amid the waters, and let it divide
> The waters from the waters . . . .
>   . . . God said
> Be gathered now ye waters under heaven
> Into one place, and let dry land appear.
> Immediately the mountains huge appear
> Emergent, and their broad bare backs upheave

Into the clouds, their tops ascend the sky . . . .
        . . . Let the earth
Put forth the verdant grass . . . .
He scarce had said, when the bare earth, till then
Desert and bare, unsightly, unadorned,
Brought forth the tender grass whose verdure clad
Her universal face with pleasant green . . .
        . . . last
Rose as in dance the stately trees, and spread
Their branches hung with copious fruit . . . .
And God created the great whales . . . .
        . . . there leviathan
Hugest of living creatures, on the deep
Stretched like a promontory sleeps or swims,
And seems a moving land, and at his gills
Draws in, and at his trunk spouts out a sea.
Mean while the tepid caves, and fens and shores
Their brood as numerous hatch, from the egg that soon
Bursting with kindly rupture forth disclosed
Their callow young . . . .[13]

The verdure, the desert, the ascending mountains, the
adorning and dressing of nature — these are common
images in Pope's pastoral scene-painting. But Milton's
prolific oxymoron, the dancing trees, the whale, the egg,
the constant shifting of land and sea, firmament and flood,
though they have dim and parallel echoes in Pope's earlier
works, are all most immediately and authentically
reproduced in Dulness's anarchic 'new world'.

If the *Messiah* or *Windsor-Forest* cannot legitimize *The
Dunciad*'s excesses, *Paradise Lost* certainly can. Pope's
perversity is a close imitation of Milton's representation of
divine creative power. And more. *The Dunciad*'s Miltonic
images are also the images of imperialist apologia. The
familiar oceans and rivers of the *concordia discors* find
new bounds in *The Dunciad*'s Miltonic creation scenes;
lands shift even more dramatically than the 'verdant Isles'
and fantastic 'floating Forests' of earlier pastorals, or than

the moving whale — mammoth emblem of maritime conquest. In fact, *The Dunciad*'s whales and dolphins, though they sport in the woods and the skies, come directly from contemporary imperialist panegyric.[14] And those woods, too, as we have seen, can serve as a trope for the displaced energies of mercantile expansion. The forests of Windsor, suddenly animated, rush into the Thames to bear the culture of the *pax Britannica* to the New World. In *The Dunciad*'s new world as well, forests provide a focal point for the dynamism of the scene; they seem to lead the 'mazy dance' that characterizes Dulness's kingdom. All the essential images of expansionist ideology are implicit in the new pastoral of *The Dunciad*, but stripped of their apologist context and their imperialist referent and thus 'floating' free of the explicit meanings associated with them in earlier poems. The forests of *Windsor* are liberated in *The Dunciad*, and their dancing is the sign of an ultimate, enthusiastic collaboration, both with the creator and with the naval power of the imperialist state, a collaboration even fuller and more fantastic than that of Burlington's 'willing woods'. The issue here is not so much the fact that Pope quotes himself, or that he alludes to Milton; these passages can all be traced beyond *Paradise Lost* to the gardens of Alcinous in the *Odyssey*, to Virgil's *Eclogues* and to the *Mosella* of Ausonius, as well as to other contemporary works by Dryden, Congreve, Marvell and Oldham.[15] But the specific character of this intertextuality — the essential similarity of *The Dunciad*'s mad, mazy and amoral imagery with that of these passages of legitimate pastoral scene-painting — makes Dulness's empire seem more like a perfect fulfilment of Pope's pastoral vision than a corrupt and pernicious deviation.

Of course *The Dunciad*'s pastorals are corrupt according to one kind of reading: Pope's note has already supplied the evidence for that assessment. These scenes are deliberately grotesque, perverse and absurd; they directly invert natural order; and like the commodity catalogues, they are anarchic, indiscriminate and fundamentally amoral. Indeed, as we have seen, the 'new world' of Book III is prefaced by a catalogue of symptomatic disorder: 'Gods, imps, and monsters, music, rage, and mirth'. Pastoral convention is corrupted by the language of commodification at this point in the poem. Just as in *The Rape of the Lock* and *Windsor-Forest* we saw the vistas of pastoral scene-painting transformed into the set-pieces of 'glitt'ring Spoil' and the lists of imperial products translated into the creatures of the sylvan war, so in *The Dunciad* we can find the amorality of commodification realized in the landscape of Dulness's empire. Reread in this way, as a painting of the scene of capitalist culture, *The Dunciad*'s pastoral teaches us to see that culture's grotesquery, its amorality and its inherent perversions of traditional systems of meaning and order.

In a sense we have already learned this lesson, however. The perversion that seems specific to *The Dunciad* is built into Pope's pastoral at its earliest appearances. True pastoral scene-painting, as *To Burlington* demonstrates, is already inherently constituted by the premises of inversion and collaboration that *The Dunciad* takes to their logical conclusion. In this respect, the transformed landscape of Burlington's 'Imperial Works' is the equivalent of *The Dunciad*'s landscape of capitalist culture: both are new worlds generated by the energies of a new mode of production. In other words, the attack on capitalism in *The Dunciad* emerges from the language, the materials and the ideological mechanisms of capitalism itself; indeed those mechanisms make Pope's invective possible by providing the formal terms of representation: oxymoron, inversion, collaboration and perverse juxtaposition.

But if *The Dunciad*'s pastoral embodies the perversions of capitalism, it also indicates its fertility at this stage in its history. No other work in Pope's corpus has been credited with the same degree of vitality, disruptive exuberance and inventive enthusiasm as *The Dunciad*.[16] This energy is most often located in the scatological epic games of Book II and in the two pastoral descriptions of the mad disorder of Dulness's empire that we have isolated for discussion here. But we can see it as well in the excessive incongruities and the fantastic conjunctions of the poem's catalogue rhetoric, and, perhaps most clearly, in the allusion to *Paradise Lost*, which serves as both signal and source for *The Dunciad*'s special vitality. Pope derives his image of Dulness's empire from the most profuse, prolific picture of unrestrained creative energy in his literary culture, and he selects for special reference those passages in Milton that stand out for their excessiveness, their unexpectedness, their power to amaze: the trees in stately dance, the whale like a moving land and the egg hatching a numerous brood to populate the earth. The attack on amorality in this poem, then, is balanced by a reciprocal enactment of creative vitality, even of fertile regeneration;[17] and the fear of disorder is countered by an equivalent, unconscious celebration of a new kind of order, a wholly 'new world'. Perhaps we can see in this ambivalence the problematic structure of Pope's personal relationship with the printing industry, where his consistent invective against materialism is countered by an energetic and successful engagement in commercial money-making.

III

Despite the dynamism and profusion that we have documented thus far in *The Dunciad*, and despite the fact that the climax of Pope's fantasy of the coming of the kingdom of Dulness is a 'new world to Nature's laws unknown' full of perverse and unbounded energy, the moment of the apocalypse itself is signalled by silence, by the cessation of activity, conflict and movement. *The Dunciad* ends twice, perhaps even three times, as if Pope were obsessively re-telling the same paradoxical silencing that he sees in capitalist cultural fertility. The first ending is the one we now usually read, the ending of the whole revised poem, after the incorporation of the *New Dunciad* as Book IV.

Dulness yawns, 'All Nature nods' (605) and the whole of English culture dozes off:

> In vain, in vain — the all-composing Hour
> Resistless falls: The Muse obeys the Pow'r.
> She comes! she comes! the sable Throne behold
> Of *Night* Primaeval, and of *Chaos* old!
> . . .
> Lo! thy dread Empire, CHAOS! is restor'd;
> Light dies before thy uncreating word:
> Thy hand, great Anarch! lets the curtain fall;
> And Universal Darkness buries All.
>
> ([B] IV, 627–56)

This last section is a revision of the closing lines of Book III in the original, shorter version of the poem as it first appeared in 1728. There the anti-logos — the inversion of God's creating words 'Let there be light' — is even more explicit:

> Then, when these signs declare the Mighty Year;
> When the dull Stars roll round, and re-appear.
> Let there be darkness! (thy dread pow'r shall say)
> All shall be darkness, as it ne'er were Day;
> Thy hand great Dulness! lets the curtain fall,
> And universal Dulness cover all.
>
> ([A] III, 335–56nn.)

The same moment of stillness occurs at the conclusion of Book II, which ends with a sleeping contest that anticipates the universal sleep of Book IV: 'And all was hush'd, as Folly's self lay dead' ([B] II, 418). This cessation of activity directly contradicts the 'mazy dance' and the gaudy 'new worlds' that we have been taught to associate with Dulness's kingdom in the body of the poem. Indeed, 'CHAOS' seems to have two distinct meanings: change and stasis,/energy and debility, dynamism and tranquillity.

This problematic image of tranquillity has a history of its own. 'Universal Darkness' comes with the final yawn, which spread throughout English culture:

More had she spoke, but yawn'd — All Nature nods:
What Mortal can resist the Yawn of Gods?
. . .
Lost was the Nation's Sense, nor could be found,
While the long solemn Unison went round:
Wide, and more wide, it spread o'er all the realm;
Ev'n Palinurus nodded at the Helm.

([B] IV, 605—14)

These lines reproduce the spreading sleep that concludes
Book II in an anticipation of the apocalypse of Book IV:

Who sate the nearest, by the words o'ercome,
Slept first; the distant nodded to the hum.
Then down are roll'd the books; stretch'd o'er 'em lies
Each gentle clerk, and mutt'ring seals his eyes.
As what a Dutchman plumps into the lakes,
One circle first, and then a second makes;
What Dulness dropt among her sons imprest
Like motion from one circle to the rest;
So from the mid-most the nutation spreads
Round and more round, o'er all the sea of heads.

([B] II, 401—10)

The image of the spreading ripple on the tranquil lake is a
central one for *The Dunciad*, but it spreads throughout
Pope's poetic corpus as well. It comes from the early
Temple of Fame, from a passage that Pope adapts from
Chaucer. The 'various sounds' — lies, rumours, news — that
fly up to Fame's temple spread through the air:

As on the smooth Expanse of Chrystal Lakes,
The sinking Stone at first a circle makes;
The trembling Surface, by the Motion stir'd,
Spreads in a second Circle, then a third;
Wide, and more wide, the floating Rings advance,
Fill all the wat'ry Plain, and to the Margin dance.

(436—41)

This version of the image of the spreading ripple innocently illustrates the conjunction of dynamism and tranquillity that we have been labouring to uncover in *The Dunciad*; it joins perfect peacefulness with yet another 'mazy dance'. Here we have at once, in a kind of metaphoric oxymoron, both the dancing trees and the universal sleep of Pope's final apocalyptic vision.

Why does this ambivalent image of energy and stasis seem to carry so much significance in Pope's corpus? Perhaps the best explanation is yet another intertextual reference, this time from the *Essay on Man*. Pope first parodied the spreading ripple image of *The Temple of Fame* in 1728, in Book II of the original version of *The Dunciad*. He seems to have taken his cue from an earlier obscene parody of the *Temple*, *Aesop at the Bear Garden* (1715):

> *As on the smooth Expance of Chrystal Lakes,*
> *The sinking Stone at first a Circle makes;*
> So from a House of Office o'er a Lake,
> A T——d falls down, and does a Circle make.
> *The trembling Surface by the Motion stir'd*
> *Spreads in a second Circle, then a third;*
> *Wide and more wide the Excrements advance,*
> *Fill all the watry Place, and to the Margin dance.*[18]

In 1741 in the *New Dunciad*, Pope repeated the parody; in 1743 he included both versions, in Books II and IV of the final complete poem.

Between these parodies, however, in 1734, he produced yet another spreading ripple image:

> Self-love but serves the virtuous mind to wake,
> As the small pebble stirs the peaceful lake;
> The centre mov'd, a circle strait succeeds,
> Another still, and still another spreads,
> Friend, parent, neighbour, first it will embrace,
> His country next, and next all human race,
> Wide and more wide, th'o'erflowings of the mind
> Take ev'ry creature in, of ev'ry kind;

Earth smiles around, with boundless bounty blest,
And Heav'n beholds its image in his breast.

(IV, 363–72)

This passage is the apocalypse of the *Essay on Man*, the point at which Pope projects a millennium of perfect order and hierarchy, 'one close system of Benevolence' (IV, 358), inaugurated by self-love and ensured by man's acceptance of his place in the chain of being. This system is, in fact, the only heaven that the poem offers, a heaven on earth for the virtuous, who thus receive 'the bliss that fills up all the mind' (IV, 344). The result is 'boundless bounty', a new world that joins prosperity and peace, the energy of aggressive self-love and the stasis of abstract truth and categorical morality. The image of the spreading ripple on the peaceful lake gives us a bridge from one apocalypse to the other: *The Dunciad* condemns capitalist expansion through the same ambivalent evocation of tranquillity that serves in the *Essay on Man* as the summary image of Pope's problematic moral rationale for a capitalist system. In other words, the *Essay on Man* ends with the same image as *The Dunciad* because it, too, records the coming of the millennium of capitalist prosperity. In both poems the spreading ripple represents this millennium as the supersession of dynamism by stasis.

The image of stasis is also in part derived from *Windsor-Forest*. That poem too obsessively ends twice, or rather repeats its image of apocalypse in two parallel passages near its conclusion. Whereas Dulness, the Mighty Mother of the new British empire, recites the anti-logos 'Let there be Darkness', in *Windsor-Forest* Queen Anne has the equivalent lines:

At length great ANNA said — Let Discord cease!
She said, the World obey'd, and all was *Peace*!

(327–8)

In the 1712 manuscript version of the poem, this line resembles Dulness's anti-logos even more closely: '*Let there be peace* — she said, and all was *peace*.'[19] A few lines later, Father Thames, arising in response, speaks with a similar tranquillizing effect:

> . . . the Winds forget to roar,
> And the hush'd Waves glide softly to the Shore.
>
> (353—4)

In discussing *The Rape of the Lock* I suggested that we could read the operations of 'True Wit' as imperial expansion by seeing in the dressing of Belinda the fantasy of the accumulation of mercantile spoils. Here we can read Queen Anne as the Mighty Mother of *The Dunciad*, and the *pax Britannica* as the coming of the kingdom of Dulness, the 'universal Darkness' of Pope's final apocalypse. This reading helps to explain the paradoxical stasis with which *The Dunciad* ends. In *Windsor-Forest* we saw that stasis as the ideological construct of imperial peace, a tranquillity ironically constituted by violence. The silence that concludes *The Dunciad*'s description of capitalist accumulation and cultural transformation is an unconscious parallel to the ideology of the *pax Britannica*, a tranquillity ironically constituted by dynamism. *The Dunciad* too sees the triumph of mercantile capitalism in terms of silence and peace. Despite its attack on the commodification of literary culture, then, *The Dunciad* represents one of the period's most detailed expressions in poetic form of the workings of capitalist ideology, and it enacts that ideology's deepest and most essential contradiction.

The actual place of imperialism in the poem itself gives some indication of the complexity of this contradiction. As we have seen, one aspect of *The Dunciad*'s representation of the final peace that closes the curtain on English culture is a local satire on Walpole's pacific foreign policy: the navies that 'yawn'd for Orders on the Main' ([B] IV, 618). We know from the political programme of the Opposition that this kind of attack implicitly indicates a demand for a more aggressive imperialism — in short, more military support for English trade, more commercial success, more accumulation, more of all the evils of acquisition and commodification that ground the poem's satire. *The Dunciad* sums up its attack on capitalism by urging a more energetic mercantile capitalist expansion. Pope, of course, is blissfully unaware of the radical incompatibility between his concluding gibe at Walpole and the body of the poem, just as he is unable to see the intimate connections of capitalism and imperialism. In fact, he uses the one against the other in the last lines of *The Dunciad* by exploiting the ambiguous status that peace has attained in his corpus. At this point in Pope's poetry, peace can mean both violence and silence, both the beginning of English culture and the end. In *Windsor-Forest* the implicit violence of imperialism is concealed by the silence of the *pax Britannica*, and this dual structure generates the hopeful new beginning of an expansionist ideology. In *The Dunciad* the violent energy of the dunces is subsumed by an incongruous stasis that serves to deny the progressive vitality of capitalism, to repudiate its hold on the future 'new world' of English culture as well as on the poet's own energetic production. This peace indicates an end of English culture in its traditional forms, but it is also a signal and negative gauge of a new beginning, a new *locus* of cultural fertility. In adding the incidental allusion to Walpole's peace to the image of cultural closure, Pope simultaneously — but by another, incongruous route — attacks the dunces for what he sees as the impending failure of English imperialism. Imperialism thus becomes a bludgeon against capitalism, and capitalism in turn serves as the scapegoat for imperialism, syphoning off all the dehumanizing effects of fetishism to leave the English empire pure, uncompromised and ideal. The resultant contradiction is a perfect rendering of the ideological position of Pope's poetic corpus: mercantile capitalism signals both the death of English culture and its rebirth.

The Dunciad's 'new world', where 'other planets circle other suns', is a perverse and enthusiastic emblem of this rebirth, of the imperialist new worlds we have discovered elsewhere in Pope's poetry. These new worlds appear in the *Essay on Criticism*'s matching images of the voyages of discovery and individual creative genius:

> Hail *Bard Triumphant*! . . .
> Nations *unborn* your mighty Names shall sound,
> And Worlds applaud that must not yet be *found*!
>
> (189—94)

> Where a *new World* leaps out at his command,
> And ready Nature waits upon his Hand.
>
> (486—7)

They figure in *Windsor-Forest*'s fantasy of the *pax Britannica*:

> Oh stretch thy Reign, fair *Peace*! from Shore to Shore,
> Til Conquest cease, and Slav'ry be no more:
> . . .
> *Peru* once more a Race of Kings behold,
> And other *Mexico's* be roof'd with Gold.
>
> (407—12)

And they recur even in the *Essay on Man*'s evocation of the impenetrability of the universe to human reason:

> He, who thro' vast immensity can pierce,
> See worlds on worlds compose one universe,
> Observe how system into system runs,
> What other planets circle other suns,
> What vary'd being peoples ev'ry star,
> May tell why Heav'n has made us as we are.
>
> (I, 23—8)

These new worlds separately demonstrate the effects that *The Dunciad*'s combine. Like the *Essay on Criticism*, *The Dunciad* contains a new world of artistic invention and aesthetic excess — in the virtuoso prosodic and semantic performances of the commodity catalogue and in the fantastic devices of contemporary theatre. Like that of *Windsor-Forest*, the new pastoral of *The Dunciad* represents the fertile new land of mercantile expansion, including even the seas, whales, woods and islands of naval supremacy. And like the 'other planets' of the *Essay on Man, The Dunciad*'s new world suggests a vast unaccountability beyond human control, an unknown system whose limits have not yet been tried.

One of the sources of these new worlds is the Galilean passage in *Paradise Lost*, when Satan throws himself down through the firmament to this world:

> Amongst innumerable stars, that shone
> Stars distant, but nigh hand seemed other worlds,
> Or other worlds they seemed, or happy isles.[20]

The fantasies of conquest and accumulation, the implicit tragedy and the concealed brutality of imperial expansion in *Windsor*, and the grotesque dynamism and inverted fertility of *The Dunciad* are both, in different ways, informed by Milton's epic. For Milton these 'other worlds' join Galileo's opening of the science of astronomy for intellectual conquest, Satan's own tragic and brutal individualist voyage of exploration and the final human challenge that confronts Adam and Eve when they are expelled from Paradise and 'The world was all before them.' Combined with the extravagant fertility of the 'new world' that *The Dunciad* derives from the creation scene of *Paradise Lost*, these informing Miltonic images figure the opening out of a cultural vista, the initiation of a new history of human individualism. On one hand, *The Dunciad* claims to invert this precedent — to replace Milton's new beginning with closure. But the Kingdom of Dulness is not simply a parody of Milton's new world, whatever Pope may have intended. The poem faithfully reproduces Milton's 'other worlds', though with a bitter ambivalence and a complex perversity, indicating in the very context of its condemnation the fulfilment of Milton's own vision of the progressive energy of bourgeois culture.

IV

The juxtaposition of *Windsor-Forest* and *The Dunciad*
enables us to read *Windsor-Forest* — the period's best
known encomium on the rise of the English empire — as
an exposure of the violence of accumulation in imperialist
culture, and *The Dunciad* — Pope's most thorough indictment of the commodification of literature, art and morality
itself — as a celebration of the prolific energies of early
English capitalism. The anarchic 'new world' of the later
poem, read back into the balanced pastoral of the earlier,
exposes the formal perversions implicit in those scenes.
Likewise, *The Dunciad*'s grotesque mechanical cataloguing
of the products of the printing industry — 'Journals,
Medleys, Merc'ries, Magazines' — opens up the catalogue
of imperial products to a special scrutiny. And reciprocally, *Windsor-Forest*'s catalogues tie listing rhetoric to
acquisition in such a way that *The Dunciad*'s wilder and
less specifically labelled catalogues can be linked to
capitalist accumulation. Because the pastoral scenes in
Windsor-Forest uncover the connection between pastoral
and commodity, we can more readily see the basis of
commodity fetishism behind *The Dunciad*'s anarchic 'new
world'. But that 'new world' in addition bears within it
Windsor-Forest's generative and celebratory pastoral vision
of cultural expansion.

If *Windsor-Forest* reveals the contradictory structure
of imperialist ideology, then, *The Dunciad* uncovers the
parallel problematic of capitalism. Here is a historical
insight beyond the capacities of either work alone, and
equally beyond the conscious perception of their author.
Windsor-Forest celebrates imperialism, *The Dunciad*
attacks capitalism, but their inter-referentiality shows that
their topic, like their apocalypse, is the same: that
capitalism and imperialism are part of the same historical
construct, and that both turn on structurally homologous
contradictions. The tension of violence and cultural
expansion, fertility and the fetishization of the com-

modity, the early energies of a new mode of production and the power and violence through which it is institutionalized — these are the parallel paradoxes of Pope's major poems.

The conjunction of *Windsor-Forest* and *The Dunciad* supplies another kind of lesson — an indication of the nature of ideological critique and its relation both to stable, determinate textual 'meaning' and also to the process of history that always provides its ultimate point of reference. *Windsor-Forest* serves as our *locus* for the rhetoric of cultural expansion, and from its perspective we can see through the simple invective of *The Dunciad* to the problematic conjunction of fertility and corruption in that poem. And yet as we have found in our reading of *Windsor-Forest*, that work in itself also problematizes the *pax Britannica*, so that what we take as a simple formal and ideological origin is already undermined. Similarly, *The Dunciad* serves in part as the basis for a rereading of *Windsor-Forest*; its wild incongruities help reveal more clearly the implicit perversions in *Windsor-Forest*'s decorous *concordia discors*. And yet my reading here claims that *The Dunciad* is not perverse at all — that it is the legitimate celebratory pastoral scene to which *Windsor-Forest* only alludes. Both poems seem to slip further from a single, simple 'meaning' the closer we come to a definition of their ideology; or rather the act of defining their ideology serves to set them in motion, to make them dynamic. As we uncover the historical significance of these works, they become history — transitory, conditional, contingent. Their meaning, the valence of their images, even the effect of their poetry is a process rather than a fact, shifting with the point from which they are viewed, the story that they are used to tell. Just as every moment in history belongs both to the future and to the past, these poems each tell two stories and supply two meanings, depending on where we stand to read them. *Windsor-Forest* glorifies the consolidation of a new cultural coherence, but we can also read it as a lesson in the contradictions of imperialist ideology. *The Dunciad* figures forth apocalypse and cultural destruction, but we can read it as a celebration of the progressive dimension of capitalist culture. These are the two sides of eighteenth-century history; neither mutually exclusive nor seamlessly compatible, neither at one nor at war. *Windsor-Forest* and *The Dunciad* show us how to see them separately but at once. In the poles of Pope's poetic corpus, then, we can catch a glimpse of the process that constitutes ideology: the movement of history, the determining dynamism in which we can locate the meaning of Pope's poetry and make it our own.

Notes

Introduction

1 Warton, *An Essay on the Writings and Genius of Pope*, vol. I (1756; repr. New York: Garland, 1974) dedication, pp. iii—iv. Also quoted in *Pope: The Critical Heritage*, ed. John Barnard, (London: Routledge and Kegan Paul, 1973), p. 380.

2 Warton, *An Essay on the Genuis and Writings of Pope*, vol. II (1782; repr. New York: Garland, 1974), p. 409. The second volume was published with a revised title. Also quoted in Barnard, p. 521.

3 Arnold, 'The Study of Poetry', in *Essays: English and American*, ed. Charles W. Eliot (1886; repr. New York: P.F. Collier and Son, 1910), pp. 65—91. The quoted passage is from p. 84.

4 Thomas Babington Macaulay, 'The Life and Writings of Addison' (1843), in *The Works of Lord Macaulay* (London: Longmans, Green, 1866), vol. VII, pp. 112—13.

5 See, for instance, Geoffrey Tillotson, *On the Poetry of Pope* (Oxford: Clarendon Press, 1938).

6 The phrase is used by Earl R. Wasserman in *Pope's 'Epistle to Bathurst': A Critical Reading with An Edition of the Manuscripts* (Baltimore: Johns Hopkins Press, 1960), p. 14.

7 Patricia Meyer Spacks, *An Argument of Images: The Poetry of Alexander Pope* (Cambridge, Mass.: Harvard Univ. Press, 1971).

8 Douglas H. White, *Pope and the Context of Controversy: The Manipulation of Ideas in 'An Essay on Man'* (Chicago: Univ. of Chicago Press, 1970).

9 Dustin H. Griffin, *Alexander Pope: The Poet in the Poems* (Princeton: Princeton Univ. Press, 1978).

10 Thomas R. Edwards, Jr., *This Dark Estate: A Reading of Pope* (Berkeley and Los Angeles: Univ. of California Press, 1963).

11 Wallace Jackson, *Vision and Re-Vision in Alexander Pope* (Detroit: Wayne State Univ. Press, 1983).

12 Steven Shankman, *Pope's Iliad: Homer in the Age of Passion*, Princeton Essays in Literature (Princeton: Princeton Univ. Press, 1983).

13 James Reeves, *The Reputation and Writings of Alexander Pope* (London: Heinemann, 1976).

14 See, for instance, the reviews by Robert W. Uphaus in *The Eighteenth Century: A Current Bibliography*, NS 5 (1979), pp. 525–6, and by Arthur J. Weitzman in *Eighteenth-Century Studies*, 10 (1977), pp. 493–6.

Chapter 1 Imperialism and Poetic Form

1 All quotation of Pope's poetry is from the Twickenham Edition as cited below. Line numbers and, if necessary, book or epistle numbers appear in parentheses in the text. Other references to the editorial material of the Twickenham volumes are given in the notes.

   The Twickenham Edition of the Poems of Alexander Pope. Volume I: *Pastoral Poetry and An Essay on Criticism*, ed. E. Audra and Aubrey Williams (London: Methuen; New Haven: Yale Univ. Press, 1961). Volume II: *The Rape of the Lock and Other Poems*, ed. Geoffrey Tillotson (London: Methuen, 1940). Volume III, i: *An Essay on Man*, ed. Maynard Mack (London: Methuen, 1950). Volume III, ii: *Epistles to Several Persons (Moral Essays)*, ed. F.W. Bateson (London: Methuen; New Haven: Yale Univ. Press, 1951). Volume IV: *Imitations of Horace with an Epistle to Dr Arbuthnot and The Epilogue to the Satires*, ed. John Butt, 2nd edn (London: Methuen; New Haven: Yale Univ. Press, 1953). Volume V: *The Dunciad*, ed. James Sutherland (London: Methuen, 1943). Volume VII: *The Iliad of Homer*, ed. Maynard Mack (London: Methuen, 1967). Volume VIII: *The Iliad of Homer*, ed. Maynard Mack (London: Methuen, 1967).

2 Reuben Arthur Brower, *Alexander Pope: The Poetry of Allusion* (Oxford: Clarendon Press, 1959), p. 203.

3 Edward Niles Hooker, 'Pope on Wit: *The Essay on Criticism*', *The Hudson Review*, 2 (1950) pp. 84–100. Reprinted in *Essential Articles for the Study of Alexander Pope*, ed. Maynard Mack, rev. edn (Hamden, Conn.: Archon Books, 1968), pp. 185–207. The quoted passage is from p. 203.

4 Patricia Meyer Spacks, *An Argument of Images: The Poetry of Alexander Pope* (Cambridge, Mass.: Harvard Univ. Press, 1971), p. 23.

5 Thomas R. Edwards, Jr., *This Dark Estate: A Reading of Pope* (Berkeley and Los Angeles: Univ. of California Press, 1963), p. viii.

6 Martin Price, *To the Palace of Wisdom: Studies in Order and Energy from Dryden to Blake* (Garden City, NY: Doubleday, 1964), p. 163.

7 Paul Fussell, *The Rhetorical World of Augustan Humanism: Ethics and Imagery from Swift to Burke* (Oxford: Clarendon Press, 1965), pp. viii, 4—10, and *passim*.

8 For the economic background of *The Rape of the Lock*, see Louis A. Landa, 'Of silkworms and farthings and the will of God', in *Studies in the Eighteenth Century II: Essays presented at the Second David Nichol Smith Memorial Seminar*, ed. R.F. Brissenden (Toronto: Univ. of Toronto Press, 1973), pp. 259—77, and especially 'Pope's Belinda, The General Emporie of the World, and the Wondrous Worm', *South Atlantic Quarterly*, 70 (1971), pp. 215—35.

9 For an account of Pope's use of the theme of painting in his poetry, see Brower, *Alexander Pope*, pp. 52—4. Ralph Cohen provides an interesting parallel definition of the use of 'prospect technique' in Augustan poetry; see 'The Augustan mode in English poetry', in *Studies in the Eighteenth Century: Essays presented at the David Nichol Smith Memorial Seminar*, ed. R.F. Brissenden (Canberra: Australian National Univ. Press, 1968), pp. 171—92.

10 *Paradise Lost*, in *The Poems of John Milton*, ed. John Carey and Alastair Fowler (London: Longmans, 1968), II, 621.

11 J. Jocelyn, *An Essay on Money and Bullion* (1718), Classic English Works on the History and Development of Economic Thought, ed. W.E. Minchinton (Wakefield: S.R. Publishers, 1970), p. 17.

12 Alexander Catcott, *The Antiquity and Honourableness of the Practice of Merchandize* (1744), pp. 5—7. Quoted from Landa, 'Pope's Belinda', p. 222.

13 Thomas Tickell, *On the Prospect of Peace* (1713), in *The Poetical Works of Thomas Tickell* (Boston: Little, Brown, 1854), p. 27. Also cited in Landa, 'Pope's Belinda', pp. 220—1.

14 Tickell's lines 'interfered with some lines of my own in the poem called Windsor Forrest, tho' written before I saw his; I transcribe both and desire your sincere judgment whether I ought not to strike out mine, either as they seem too like his, or as they are inferior.' Pope to Caryll, 29 November 1712, in *The Correspondence of Alexander Pope*, ed. George Sherburn (Oxford: Clarendon Press, 1956), vol. I, p. 157.

15 Richard Blackmore, *Creation. A Philosophical Poem. In Seven Books* (London: 1712), book II, 760—7, p. 99. Also cited in Landa, 'Of silkworms', p. 277.

16 Daniel Defoe, *Review*, I [i.e. IX], no. 43 (8 January 1713), in *Defoe's Review, Reproduced from the Original Editions*, introd.

by Arthur Wellesley Secord (New York: Columbia Univ. Press, 1938), facs. book 22, p. 85. Also cited in Twickenham, vol. II, 119. In fact tea and coffee together are almost a synecdoche for trade in this period. See Bernard Mandeville: 'What Estates have been got by Tea and Coffee!' In *The Fable of the Bees: Or, Private Vices, Publick Benefits*, ed. F.B. Kaye (Oxford: Clarendon Press, 1924), vol. I, 359.

17 For another perspective on commodity fetishism in the poem, see C.E. Nicholson, 'A world of artefacts: *The Rape of the Lock* as social history', *Literature and History*, 5 (1979), pp. 183—93.

18 Karl Marx, *Capital*, tr. Ben Fowkes, vol. I (New York: Random House, 1977), pp. 163—77.

19 George Lichtheim, *Imperialism* (New York: Praeger, 1971), pp. 8—9.

20 For background on these matters, see Perry Anderson, *Lineages of the Absolutist State* (London: NLB, 1974), pp. 58—9; Maurice Dobb, *Studies in the Development of Capitalism*, 2nd edn (New York: International Publishers, 1963), pp. 200—10; Michael Kammen, *Empire and Interest: The American Colonies and the Politics of Mercantilism* (Philadelphia: Lippincott, 1970), pp. 6—7 and 72—3; Christopher Hill, *The Century of Revolution 1603—1714* (London: Oxford Univ. Press, 1966), pp. 265—6; D.C. Coleman, *The Economy of England 1450—1750* (London: Oxford Univ. Press, 1977), pp. 132—4 and 137—8; and W.A. Speck, *Stability and Strife: England, 1714—1760* (Cambridge, Mass.: Harvard Univ. Press, 1977), p. 127.

21 On these points, see Coleman, *Economy of England*, pp. 140—5 and 149—50; Christopher Hill, *Reformation to Industrial Revolution, 1530—1780* (New York: Pantheon, 1967), pp. 191—4; Ralph Davis, *The Rise of the Atlantic Economies* (Ithaca, NY: Cornell Univ. Press, 1973), pp. 286—7.

22 Hill, *Century of Revolution*, pp. 262—3 and *Reformation to Industrial Revolution*, pp. 185—6; Davis, *Rise of the Atlantic Economies*, pp. 258—9; Coleman, *Economy of England*, p. 143; Daniel P. Mannix, collab. Malcolm Cowley, *Black Cargoes: A History of the Atlantic Slave Trade 1518—1865* (New York: Viking, 1962), pp. 50—68.

23 Davis, *Rise of the Atlantic Economies*, pp. 264—87.

24 As Murray Krieger says, 'It is by this late date not at all original to claim that Pope's *The Rape of the Lock* is double-edged throughout, that in it he celebrates the artificial world of 18th-century social convention even as he satirizes it.' See 'The "Frail China Jar" and the Rude Hand of Chaos', *Centennial Review of Arts and Sciences*, 5 (1961), pp. 176—94; reprinted in *Essential Articles for the Study of Alexander Pope*, ed. Mack, pp. 301—19. The quoted passage appears on p. 302.

25 William Frost, 'The Rape of the Lock and Pope's Homer', Modern Language Quarterly, 8 (1947), pp. 342—54. Reprinted in Essential Articles for the Study of Alexander Pope, ed. Mack, pp. 266—83.
26 Twickenham, vol. II, p. 154n.
27 W.R. Johnson, Darkness Visible: A Study of Vergil's 'Aeneid' (Berkeley and Los Angeles: Univ. of California Press, 1976), p. 13. For a concise summary of what he calls the 'pessimistic Harvard school', see pp. 1—18.
28 Brower, Alexander Pope, p. 60.
29 Earl R. Wasserman, The Subtler Language: Critical Readings of Neoclassic and Romantic Poems (Baltimore: Johns Hopkins Press, 1959), pp. 140—1.
30 Tickell, The Royal Progress (1714), in The Poetical Works of Thomas Tickell, p. 45.
31 For another kind of analysis of the 'displacement procedures' that dominate the poem, see Sanford Budick, Poetry of Civilization: Mythopoeic Displacement in the Verse of Milton, Dryden, Pope, and Johnson (New Haven: Yale Univ. Press, 1974), pp. 113—23.
32 Georgics, IV, 176. See Twickenham, vol. I, p. 160n.
33 Edward Young, Imperium Pelagi. A Naval Lyric (1729, 2nd edn), The Merchant. An Ode on the British Trade and Navigation, in The Poetical Works of the Reverend Edward Young, LL.D. (London, 1741), vol. II, p. 74.
34 John Trenchard, Cato's Letters, no. 64 (3 February 1721), repr. in The English Libertarian Heritage From the Writings of John Trenchard and Thomas Gordon in 'The Independent Whig' and 'Cato's Letters', ed. David L. Jacobson (Indianapolis: Bobbs-Merrill, 1965), p. 146.
35 Brower, Alexander Pope, pp. 51—4.
36 Joseph Addison, The Spectator, no. 69 (19 May 1711), ed. Donald F. Bond (Oxford: Clarendon Press, 1965), vol. I, p. 296. For a semiological account of the tendency in mercantilist thought of this period to translate the 'native ground' of England into the global geography of English commerce, see James H. Bunn, 'The aesthetics of British mercantilism', New Literary History, 11 (1980), pp. 303—21.
37 Wasserman, The Subtler Language, p. 82.
38 Denham, Cooper's Hill, in The Poetical Works of Sir John Denham, ed. Theodore Howard Banks, Jr. (New Haven: Yale Univ. Press, 1928), p. 77, lines 191—2. Subsequent references will be to this edition, and line numbers will be cited parenthetically in the text.
39 For a full statement of this argument, see Wasserman, The Subtler Language, pp. 47—81.

40　Twickenham, vol. I, p. 169n.

41　*Cato's Letters*, no. 64, p. 146.

42　Young, *Imperium Pelagi*, p. 96.

43　On 'bleeding' see Wallace Jackson, *Vision and Re-Vision in Alexander Pope* (Detroit: Wayne State Univ. Press, 1983), pp. 30–2.

44　Twickenham, vol. I, p. 191n.

45　Pope to [Teresa] Blount, [6 or 13 March 1720], *Correspondence*, ed. Sherburn, vol. II, p. 38.

46　George Lillo, *The London Merchant*, ed. William H. McBurney (Lincoln, Nebr.: Univ. of Nebraska Press, 1965), III.i. 1–28.

47　Maynard Mack, 'Introduction to Alexander Pope', in *Major British Writers*, vol. I, ed. G.B. Harrison (New York: Harcourt Brace Jovanovich, 1959), pp. 749–59. Reprinted as 'Alexander Pope' in *Pope: A Collection of Critical Essays*, ed. J.V. Guerinot (Englewood Cliffs, NJ: Prentice-Hall, 1972), pp. 30–49. The quoted passage is from p. 37.

48　Walter Benjamin, 'Theses on the philosophy of history', in *Illuminations*, ed. Hannah Arendt, tr. Harry Zohn (New York: Schocken, 1969), p. 256.

Chapter 2　The 'New World' of Augustan Humanism

1　See Donald T. Siebert, Jr., 'Cibber and Satan: *The Dunciad* and civilization', *Eighteenth-Century Studies*, 10 (1976/77), pp. 203–21, esp. pp. 203–7, for an interesting survey of what he calls the 'School of Deep Intent'.

2　See Pierre Macherey, *A Theory of Literary Production*, tr. Geoffrey Wall (London: Routledge and Kegan Paul, 1978) on Jules Verne: 'It is interesting that Verne's work has a history, but it is not this aspect of his work which has been historically important' (p. 164).

3　W.A. Speck, *Stability and Strife: England, 1714–1760* (Cambridge, Mass.: Harvard Univ. Press, 1977), pp. 143–66, and H.T. Dickinson, *Liberty and Property: Political Ideology in Eighteenth-Century Britain* (New York: Holmes and Meier, 1977), pp. 163–92.

4　*The Craftsman, by Caleb d'Anvers*, no. 346, vol. 10 (London, 1737), pp. 145–6. Also cited in Speck, *Stability and Strife*, p. 158.

5　For Walpole's policies, see J.H. Plumb, *England in the Eighteenth Century* (Harmondsworth, Middlesex: Penguin, 1950), pp. 60–73, and Dickinson, *Walpole and the Whig Supremacy* (London: English Universities Press, 1973), pp. 113–39.

6　Examples range from Elwin's complaint of 'a perplexing want of precision' in *The Works of Alexander Pope*, vol. II, ed. John Wilson Croker and Whitwell Elwin (London: John Murray, 1871), p. 25, to Arthur Fenner, Jr., 'The unity of Pope's *Essay on Criticism*', *Philological Quarterly*, 39 (1960), pp. 435—56. Fenner's essay is reprinted in *Essential Articles for the Study of Alexander Pope*, ed. Maynard Mack, rev. edn (Hamden, Conn.: Archon Books, 1968), pp. 227—41.

7   'He ought to have told them [his ignorant readers] what he means by Nature, and what it is to write or to judge according to Nature.' 'Reflections . . . upon An Essay upon Criticism', in *The Critical Works of John Dennis*, ed. Edward Niles Hooker, vol. 1 (Baltimore: Johns Hopkins Press, 1939), p. 403. Also cited in Twickenham, vol. I, p. 219.

8   See William K. Wimsatt, Jr., and Cleanth Brooks, *Literary Criticism: A Short History* (New York: Random House, 1957), pp. 221—47, and Twickenham, vol. I, pp. 209—23.

9   See, for example, Edward Niles Hooker, 'Pope on Wit', *Essential Articles for the Study of Alexander Pope*, ed. Mack, and Twickenham, vol. I, pp. 209—12.

10 For an engaging and influential discussion of this issue, see William Empson, 'Wit in the *Essay on Criticism*', in *The Structure of Complex Words* (London: Chatto and Windus, 1951), pp. 84—100. Reprinted in *Essential Articles for the Study of Alexander Pope*, ed. Mack, pp. 208—26.

11 For a detailed discussion of this problem, see Twickenham, vol. I, pp. 212—19.

12 See George T. Amis, 'The structure of the Augustan couplet', *Genre*, 9 (1976), pp. 37—58, esp. pp. 55—8.

13 Hugh Kenner, 'Pope's reasonable rhymes', *ELH*, 41 (1974), pp. 74—88. See pp. 87—8.

14 For the background to these ideas, see Twickenham, vol. I, pp. 219—23, and A.O. Lovejoy, ' "Nature" as aesthetic norm', in *Essays in the History of Ideas* (Baltimore: Johns Hopkins Press, 1948), pp. 69—77, and *The Great Chain of Being: A Study of the History of an Idea* (Cambridge, Mass.: Harvard Univ. Press, 1936).

15 John Locke, *Two Treatises of Government*, ed. Thomas I. Cook (New York: Macmillan, 1947), p. 123, (*Second Treatise*, ch. 2).

16 Daniel Defoe, *Review*, IV, no. 108 (21 October 1707), *Defoe's Review, Reproduced from the Original Editions*, introd. by Arthur Wellesley Secord (New York: Columbia Univ. Press, 1938), facs. book 10, pp. 431—2.

17 See Earl R. Wassermann, *The Subtler Language: Critical Readings of Neoclassic and Romantic Poems* (Baltimore: Johns Hopkins Press, 1959), p. 113, and especially Samuel Kliger, *The Goths in England: A Study in Seventeenth and*

Eighteenth-Century Thought (Cambridge, Mass.: Harvard Univ. Press, 1952).

18   Edward Young, *Imperium Pelagi: A Naval Lyric* (1729, 2nd edn), *The Merchant. An Ode on the British Trade and Navigation*, in *The Poetical Works of the Reverend Edward Young, LL.D.* (London, 1741), p. 84.

19   See Twickenham, vol. I, p. 300.

20   Young, *Imperium Pelagi*, p. 74.

21   Philip Sidney, *An Apologie for Poetrie*, in *English Literary Criticism: The Renaissance*, ed. O.B. Hardison, Jr. (New York: Appleton-Century-Crofts, 1963), p. 104.

22   See Louis B. Wright, *Middle-Class Culture in Elizabethan England* (1935; repr. Ithaca, NY: Cornell Univ. Press, 1958), pp. 508—48.

23   Samuel Purchas, *Purchas His Pilgrimes* (London, 1625), To the Reader. Also cited in Wright, *Middle-Class Culture*, p. 539.

24   See Twickenham, vol. I, p. 249.

25   John Dryden, *Religio Laici*, in *The Works of John Dryden*, vol. II: *Poems 1681—1684*, ed. H.T. Swedenberg, Jr., and Vinton A. Dearing (Berkeley and Los Angeles: Univ. of California Press, 1972), lines 174—9.

26   The main contemporary source for these conflicts is *Narratives of the Indian Wars 1675—1699*, ed. Charles H. Lincoln (New York: Charles Scribner, 1913). For a comprehensive though judgementally prejudiced summary, see William Christie Macleod, *The American Indian Frontier* (New York: Alfred A. Knopf, 1928), pp. 193—292. A briefer account is available in John Tebbel, *The Compact History of the Indian Wars* (New York: Hawthorn Books, 1966), pp. 9—47.

27   Richard Savage, *Of Public Spirit in Regard to Public Works*, second version (1737), in *The Poetical Works of Richard Savage*, ed. Clarence Tracy (Cambridge: Cambridge Univ. Press, 1962), p. 233, lines 293—304.

28   For a discussion of the poem's treatment of animals, see Judith Shklar's essay, shortly to be published in the collection of *English Institute Essays* for 1983.

29   On this doctrine, see Louis A. Landa, 'Of silkworms and farthingales and the will of God', in *Studies in the Eighteenth Century: Essays presented at the Second David Nichol Smith Memorial Seminar*, ed. R.F. Brissenden (Toronto: Univ. of Toronto Press, 1973), pp. 259—77.

30   Daniel Defoe, *Review*, I [i.e. IX], no. 54 (3 February 1713), *Defoe's Review*, facs. book 22, p. 107.

31   See Twickenham, vol. III, i, pp. 31—2n.

32   Young, *Imperium Pelagi*, pp. 67 and 85.

33   [James Ralph], *Clarinda, Or the Fair Libertine: A Poem in*

Four Cantos (London, 1729), pp. 37—8. Quoted from Louis A. Landa, 'Pope's Belinda, the General Emporie of the World and the Wondrous Worm', *South Atlantic Quarterly*, 70 (1971), p. 223.

34   John Durant Breval, *The Art of Dress. A Poem* (London, 1717), p. 17. Also cited in Landa, 'Pope's Belinda', p. 232.

35   [Soame Jenyns], *The Art of Dancing. A Poem* (1730), in *Poems* (London, 1752), p. 7. Also cited in Landa, 'Pope's Belinda', p. 232.

36   See, for example, John Laird, *Philosophical Incursions into English Literature* (Cambridge: Univ. Press, 1946), pp. 34—51, and Reuben Arthur Brower, *Alexander Pope: The Poetry of Allusion* (Oxford: Clarendon Press, 1959), p. 209. Most critics of the poem concede its incoherence and go on from there. Martin Price, for instance, makes the typical suggesion that Pope 'is interested in something more than consistency' (*To the Palace of Wisdom: Studies in Order and Energy from Dryden to Blake* [Garden City, NY: Doubleday, 1964], p. 139). Miriam Leranbaum observes that interpretations of the poem 'are a good deal more coherent, more consistent, more fully integrated than the poem itself' (*Alexander Pope's 'Opus Magnum', 1729—1744* [Oxford: Clarendon Press, 1977], p. 38). Douglas H. White reverses the pattern by concluding with the concession: 'The fun of the *Essay on Man* is with Pope's performance, not with the validity of the philosophy' (*Pope and the Context of Controversy: The Manipulation of Ideas in 'An Essay on Man'* [Chicago: Univ. of Chicago Press, 1970], p. 193).

37   Again, see Lovejoy, *Great Chain of Being*. But see also, for a different perspective on the relation of the *Essay* to the chain of being, F.E.L. Priestley, 'Pope and the Great Chain of Being', in *Essays in English Literature from the Renaissance to the Victorian Age, Presented to A.S.P. Woodhouse*, ed. Millar MacLure and F. W. Watt (Toronto: Univ. of Toronto Press, 1964), pp. 23—28. Priestley suggests that Pope's representation of the potential dissolution of the chain shows that he does not consistently view it as an ontological category, but rather as a conditional state that must be preserved from challenge. His reading tends to support my sense that the *Essay* represents a shoring up of traditional values in the face of a simultaneous awareness of their supersession.

38   See the general argument of White's *Pope and the Context of Controversy*. But White must admit, at times, that 'Pope's position is, to be sure, not perfectly unequivocal' (p. 180).

39   The debate over the meaning of this line, carried on through editorial decisions about its punctuation, is summarized by White, *Pope and the Context of Controversy*, pp. 181—2. My

conclusions differ from White's, but the important point, from my perspective, is the problematic nature of the line. The fact that its meaning has proven so slippery in itself supports the categorical instability in the poem which my argument emphasizes.

40 White, *Pope and the Context of Controversy*, p. 191.

41 For the dichotomy between 'rigorism' and 'loose utilitarianism' − that is, between a traditional allegiance to abstract truth, ascetic ideals and categorical morality, as opposed to a concern with the circumstances and consequences of actions − see F.B. Kaye's introd. to his edition of Mandeville, *The Fable of the Bees: Or, Private Vices, Publick Benefits* (Oxford: Clarendon Press, 1924). The terms 'rigorism' and 'loose utilitarianism', which Kaye introduced, are now widely used by critics of the *Essay on Man*.

42 For another summary of the inconsistencies in the *Essay*, see Twickenham, vol. III, i, pp. xxxviii−xxxix.

43 Price remarks on the incongruity of these two historical phases: 'This ideal society gives way suddenly and mysteriously to the joint rule of Tyranny and Superstition' (*To the Palace of Wisdom*, p. 129).

44 A variety of critics have described this paradox from a variety of different perspectives. Price: 'One might say that Pope is reconciling a keen Mandevillian sense of the origin of social order with the trust in human nature that Shaftesbury shows' (*To the Palace of Wisdom*, p. 131). White: Pope 'adopts the widely known attitude of Hobbes, Mandeville, Esprit, and Le Rochefoucauld by admitting that all human actions are the product of self-love. To that attitude, however, he adds a definition of virtue that allows man to be self-loving and virtuous at the same time' (*Pope and the Context of Controversy*, p. 191). Bertrand A. Goldgar: 'on the one hand, we are told that self-love is the dominant principle in man, that the passions are all selfish, and that these passions are in a state of war. On the other hand, we are shown simultaneously that self-love and reason both have indispensable functions and can operate harmoniously' ('Pope's Theory of the Passions: the background of Epistle II of the *Essay on Man*', *Philological Quarterly*, 41 [1962], pp. 730−43, esp. p. 739).

45 Albert O. Hirschman, *The Passions and the Interests: Political Arguments for Capitalism before Its Triumph* (Princeton: Princeton Univ. Press, 1977).

46 Giambattista Vico, *The New Science* (1744), tr. Thomas Goddard Bergin and Max Howard Fisch (Ithaca, NY: Cornell Univ. Press, 1948), p. 56, pghs 132−3.

47 Joseph Addison, *The Spectator*, no. 255 (22 December 1711),

ed. Donald F. Bond (Oxford: Clarendon Press, 1965), vol. II, p. 490.

48 Mandeville, *The Fable of the Bees*, vol. I, pp. 25—6.

49 The published version of line 240 reads 'That disappoints th' effect of ev'ry vice.' For the manuscript version, consult *An Essay on Man. Reproductions of the Manuscripts in the Pierpont Morgan Library and the Houghton Library with the Printed Text of the Original Edition*, introd. Maynard Mack (Oxford: Oxford Univ. Press, 1962). The variant manuscript lines are quoted in *The Works of Alexander Pope*, vol. II, ed. Croker and Elwin, pp. 394—5, n. 7.

50 Kaye, introd. to *The Fable of the Bees*, vol. I, p. cxxv.

51 Adam Smith, *An Inquiry into the Nature and Causes of the Wealth of Nations*, ed. Edwin Cannan, 2nd edn (Chicago: Univ. of Chicago Press, 1976), vol. II, pp. 49—50.

52 Smith, *The Wealth of Nations*, vol. II, pp. 302—3.

53 Adam Smith, *Lectures on Justice, Police, Revenue and Arms*, ed. Edwin Cannan (Oxford: Clarendon Press, 1896), p. 259. Also quoted in Hirschman, *The Passions and the Interests*, pp. 106—7. Robert L. Heilbroner outlines what he calls the paradox of Smith's assumptions, the contradiction between his 'sense of confidence and promise' and the images of decline and decay that he simultaneously presents in his account of the 'deterioration of the human condition'. According to Heilbroner, Smith exhibits a profound ambivalence toward self-interest, the acquisitive impulse that generates his prediction of a prosperous future. We can compare Smith's ambivalence with Pope's. Heilbroner claims that this central contradiction in Smith's thought 'enables us to place Smith's masterpiece in its proper historical context . . . as a paradigmatic exposition of the economic and sociological thought of its time'. The *Essay on Man* occupies a similar position in the same paradigm. See 'The paradox of progress: decline and decay in *The Wealth of Nations*', in *Essays on Adam Smith*, ed. Andrew S. Skinner and Thomas Wilson (Oxford: Clarendon Press, 1975), pp. 524—39, esp. p. 536.

Chapter 3 The Ideology of Neo-classical Aesthetics

1 The 'Advertisement' is reprinted in Twickenham, vol. III, ii, pp. xviii-xx.

2 Twickenham, vol. III, ii, p. 36n.

3 This problem is also described by Peter Dixon: in the last lines of the poem Pope 'is unable to make the usual sharp contrast between his satiric victims and the entirely worthy recipient of

his verse-letter, for each individual, without exception, is controlled by his Ruling Passion.' See *The World of Pope's Satires: An Introduction to the 'Epistles' and 'Imitations of Horace'* (London: Methuen, 1968), pp. 26—7.

4 See Miriam Leranbaum, *Alexander Pope's 'Opus Magnum', 1729—1744* (Oxford: Clarendon Press, 1977), pp. 75—81.

5 John E. Sitter defines the same phenomenon, though he does not read the poem as therefore incoherent, when he describes the epistle as primarily a lesson in humility and self-knowledge at the expense of the assertions of determinacy in the short ruling passion passage. See 'The argument of Pope's *Epistle to Cobham*', *Studies in English Literature*, 17 (1977), pp. 435—49.

6 J.G.A. Pocock, *The Machiavellian Moment: Florentine Political Thought and the Atlantic Republican Tradition* (Princeton: Princeton Univ. Press, 1975), pp. 462 and 465.

7 Leranbaum, *Alexander Pope's 'Opus Magnum'*, pp. 71—5.

8 Male readers have not always registered this contempt. Surprisingly many critics have commended Pope for the 'compassion', the 'pathos' or the 'fundamental[ly] human' value of his treatment of women in the poem. See, for example, Thomas R. Edwards, Jr., *This Dark Estate: A Reading of Pope* (Berkeley and Los Angeles: Univ. of California Press, 1963), pp. 74—5; Sitter, 'The argument of Pope's *Epistle to Cobham*', p. 78; and Maynard Mack, ' "Wit and poetry and Pope": some observations on his imagery', in *Pope and His Contemporaries: Essays presented to George Sherburn*, ed. James L. Clifford and Louis A. Landa (Oxford: Clarendon Press, 1949), p. 35.

9 Carole Fabricant, 'Binding and Dressing Nature's Loose Tresses: the ideology of Augustan landscape design', *Studies in Eighteenth-Century Culture*, 8 (1979), pp. 109—35.

10 John Berger, 'Past seen from a possible future', in *The Look of Things: Essays by John Berger*, ed. Nikos Stangos (New York: Viking, 1974), p. 215. Also cited in Fabricant, 'Binding and Dressing Nature's Loose Tresses', pp. 114—15.

11 *The Fable of the Bees*, vol. I, p. 106.

12 *The Fable of the Bees*, vol. I, pp. 355—6. Two notable readings of *To Bathurst* reject the notion of Mandevillianism. Earl R. Wasserman sees a theological unity in the poem by which the 'extremes in man' are reconciled according to a providential purpose: Mandeville's concern is the material good of society, Pope's the eternal good of mankind; see *Pope's 'Epistle to Bathurst': A Critical Reading with an Edition of the Manuscripts* (Baltimore: Johns Hopkins Press, 1960), pp. 33—40. Paul J. Alpers similarly argues that the poem is anti-Mandevillian in 'insisting on non-economic, moral criteria to judge the state'; see 'Pope's *To Bathurst* and the Mandevillian state',

ELH, 25 (1958), pp. 23—42. Reprinted in *Essential Articles for the study of Alexander Pope*, ed. Maynard Mack, rev. edn (Hamden, Conn.: Archon Books, 1968), pp. 476—97; the quoted passage appears on p. 489. Both of these readings emphasize that rigoristic force of the poem, in opposition to earlier arguments that assign to it a relatively simply utilitarianism. Clearly any adequate analysis of *To Bathurst* must account for the dynamic tension between these two aspects.

13   For the poem's many connections with the South Sea Bubble, see Vincent Carretta, 'Pope's *Epistle to Bathurst* and the South Sea Bubble', *Journal of English and Germanic Philology*, 77 (1978), pp. 212—31.

14   For a full account of the poem's connection with the financial revolution, see Howard Erskine-Hill, 'Pope and the financial revolution', in *Writers and their Background: Alexander Pope*, ed. Peter Dixon (Athens: Ohio Univ. Press, 1972), pp. 200—29.

15   For this point, see Dixon, *The World of Pope's Satires*, pp. 195—6.

16   Erskine-Hill, 'Pope and the financial revolution', p. 224.

17   Reuben Arthur Brower describes the problem of the poem this way: 'we must admire Pope for an instinctive common-sense inconsistency, for insisting that moral effort was still necessary in spite of the logic of his philosophic position. In a world where nature's laws work without fail to balance waste with miserliness, there would of course be little point in exhorting men to imitate the Man of Ross, or to adopt the golden mean in managing their wealth' (*Alexander Pope: The Poetry of Allusion* [Oxford: Clarendon Press, 1959], pp. 259—60).

18   Howard Erskine-Hill, *The Social Milieu of Alexander Pope: Lives, Example and the Poetic Response* (New Haven: Yale Univ. Press, 1975), pp. 15—41.

19   See Dixon, *The World of Pope's Satires*, pp. 61—2.

20   Richard Savage, *Of Public Spirit in Regard to Public Works*, pp. 224—5, lines 15—18. This poem plays upon Pope's imperialist and capitalist panegyrics in a variety of interesting ways.

21   Daniel Defoe, *A Tour Thro' the whole Island of Great Britain (1724—26)*, introd. G.D.H. Cole (London: Peter Davies, 1927), vol. II, pp. 527, 528, 535, and vol. I, p. 252.

22   Pocock, *The Machiavellian Moment*, pp. 464—5.

23   See Twickenham, vol. III, ii, pp. 148—9.

24   For a discussion of the significance of woman as the central figure of 'a system in which sex, land, morality, and their economic substructure combine in such a way that . . . each can only be understood in combination with the others', see James G. Turner, 'The sexual politics of landscape: images of Venus in eighteenth-century English poetry and landscape gardening',

Studies in Eighteenth-Century Culture, 11 (1982), pp. 343—66.
The quoted passage appears on p. 360.

25 Pope's note to the last lines of the conclusion shows that he was
    aware of current public works projects, and critical of their
    shoddy and corrupt execution. Burlington is the ideal alterna-
    tive to these misconceived p.ojects. See Twickenham, vol. III,
    ii, pp. 150—1n.

26 'This vision of useful art is perhaps the most "Augustan" passage
    Pope ever wrote . . . We respond not to "fact" but to the intel-
    ligent courage that rises above the merely factual to assert
    imaginatively the permanent possibility of goodness in the
    human condition' (Edwards, This Dark Estate, pp. 71—2).

27 Oliver Goldsmith, The Deserted Village, in The Poems of
    Thomas Gray, William Collins, Oliver Goldsmith, ed. Roger
    Lonsdale (London: Longman, 1969), pp. 693—4, lines 407—
    28. The last couplet here is attributed to Samuel Johnson.

28 Dixon, The World of Pope's Satires, p. 61.

Chapter 4 The New Pastoral — Capitalism and Apocalypse

1 Pope to Swift, 14 September 1725, The Correspondence of
   Alexander Pope, ed. George Sherburn (Oxford: Clarendon
   Press, 1956), vol. II, pp. 321—2.

2 Twickenham, vol. V, p. ix.

3 Reginald Harvey Griffith, Alexander Pope: A Bibliography,
   vol. II, (Austin: Univ. of Texas, 1927), p. xlvii. Also quoted in
   James A. Winn, 'On Pope, printers and publishers', Eighteenth-
   Century Life, 6 (1981), pp. 93—102, p. 94.

4 For Pope's relations with his publishers, see Winn, 'On Pope,
   printers and publishers'.

5 For extensive data on Pope's subscriptions, see Pat Rogers,
   'Pope and his subscribers', Publishing History, 3 (1978), pp.
   7—36.

6 Rogers, 'Pope and his subscribers', p. 30.

7 Pope to Allen [14 July 1741], Correspondence, vol. IV, p.
   350. Also quoted in Winn, 'On Pope, printers and publishers',
   p. 100.

8 Irvin Ehrenpreis, 'The style of sound: the literary value of
   Pope's versification', in The Augustan Milieu: Essays Presented
   to Louis A. Landa, ed. Henry Knight Miller, Eric Rothstein and
   G.S. Rousseau (Oxford: Clarendon Press, 1970), pp. 232—46, esp.
   pp. 235—6. Ehrenpreis sees this listing rhetoric as a defect,
   arguing that it prevents 'the progress of an argument, a narrative,
   a descriptive plan, or any other scheme derived from meaning'
   (p. 236n).

9   See Georg Lukács, *History and Class Consciousness: Studies in Marxist Dialectics*, tr. Rodney Livingstone (Cambridge, Mass.: MIT Press, 1971), pp. 83—110.
10 Twickenham, vol. V, [A] I, 71n.
11 Twickenham, vol. V, p. 224.
12 *The Art of Sinking in Poetry: A Critical Edition*, ed. Edna Leake Steeves (New York: King's Crown Press, 1952), pp. 48—9.
13 *Paradise Lost*, VII, 261—420.
14 Edward Young's praise of English mercantile supremacy makes precisely this use of the images of the whale and dolphin:

>   Let the proud Brothers of the Land,
>   Smile at our Rocks and *barren* Strand,
> Not *such* the Sea: Let *Fohe*'s antient Line
>   Vast *Tracts*, and ample *Beings* vaunt;
>   The Camel *low*, *small* Elephant;
> O *Britain!* the *Leviathan* is Thine.

>   *Leviathan!* whom *Nature*'s Strife
>   Brought forth her largest Piece of Life;
> He *sleeps* an Isle! his sports the Billow warm!
>   Dreadful *Leviathan!* thy Spout
>   Invades the Skies; the Stars are out:
> He drinks a *River*, and ejects a *Storm*.

>   . . .
>   The *Whale* (for late I sung his Praise)
>   Pours *grateful* Lustre on my Lays;
> How smiles *Arion*'s Friend ['The Dolphin'] with *partial*
>   Beams?

(*Imperium Pelagi. A Naval Lyric* (1729, 2nd edn), *The Merchant. An Ode on the British Trade and Navigation*, in *The Poetical Works of the Reverend Edward Young, LL.D.* [London, 1741], pp. 87 and 102).
15 See Twickenham, vol. I, p. 79n, 169n, and vol. II, p. 251n; and Reuben Arthur Brower, *Alexander Pope: The Poetry of Allusion* (Oxford: Clarendon Press, 1959), pp. 50—3.
16 See Peter Dixon, *The World of Pope's Satires: An Introduction to the 'Epistles' and 'Imitations of Horace'* (London: Methuen, 1968), pp. 200—2; Emrys Jones, 'Pope and Dullness', Chatterton Lecture on an English Poet, in *Proceedings of the British Academy*, 54 (London: Oxford Univ. Press, 1970), pp. 231—64; and especially Howard Erskine-Hill, 'The "New World" of Pope's *Dunciad*', *Renaissance and Modern Studies*, 6 (1962), pp. 49—67.
17 For a reading of the images of regeneration in the poem through

a description of its sacramental form, see Sanford Budick, *Poetry of Civilization: Mythopoeic Displacement in the Verse of Milton, Dryden, Pope, and Johnson* (New Haven: Yale Univ. Press, 1974), pp. 134—55.

18 *AEsop at the Bear-Garden: A Vision* (1715), repr. in *Popeiana I: Early Criticism, 1711 to 1716* (New York: Garland, 1975), p. 30.

19 For this manuscript line, as cited from Warburton, see *The Works of Alexander Pope*, vol. I, ed. John Wilson Croker and Whitwell Elwin (London: John Murray, 1871), p. 360, n.3.

20 *Paradise Lost*, III, 565—7.

Index